ZENTASTIC

Mandala's

I0468934

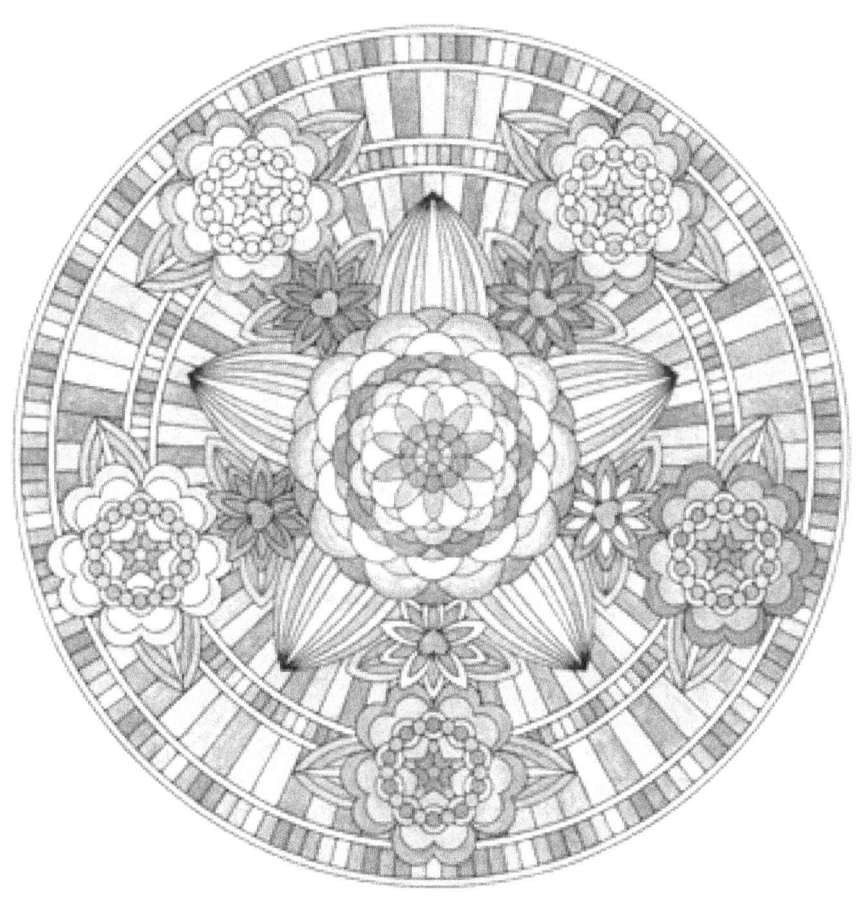

Color Yourself Calm
Created By Lisa Brando

ZENTASTIC
Mandala's

This coloring book is designed to help you reduce stress, anxiety and worry. All you need to do is grab some colored pencils, markers or crayons sit back, relax and just let your mind free.

Most of all, have fun!

Lisa Brando xoxo :)

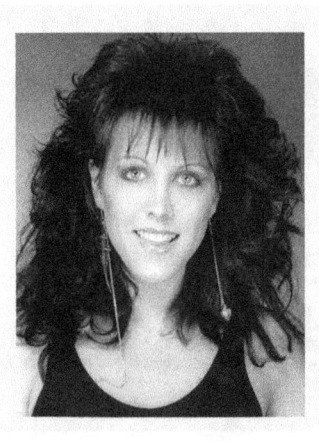

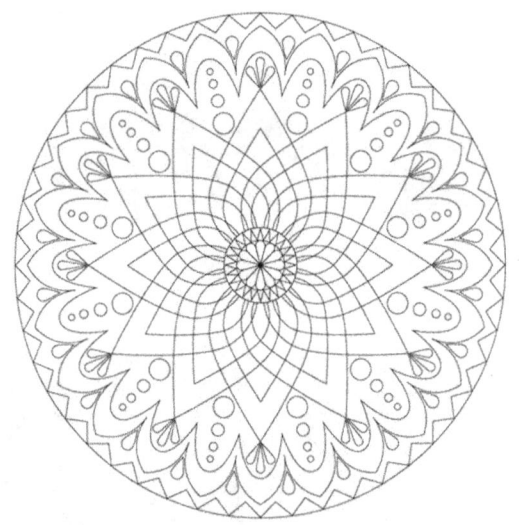

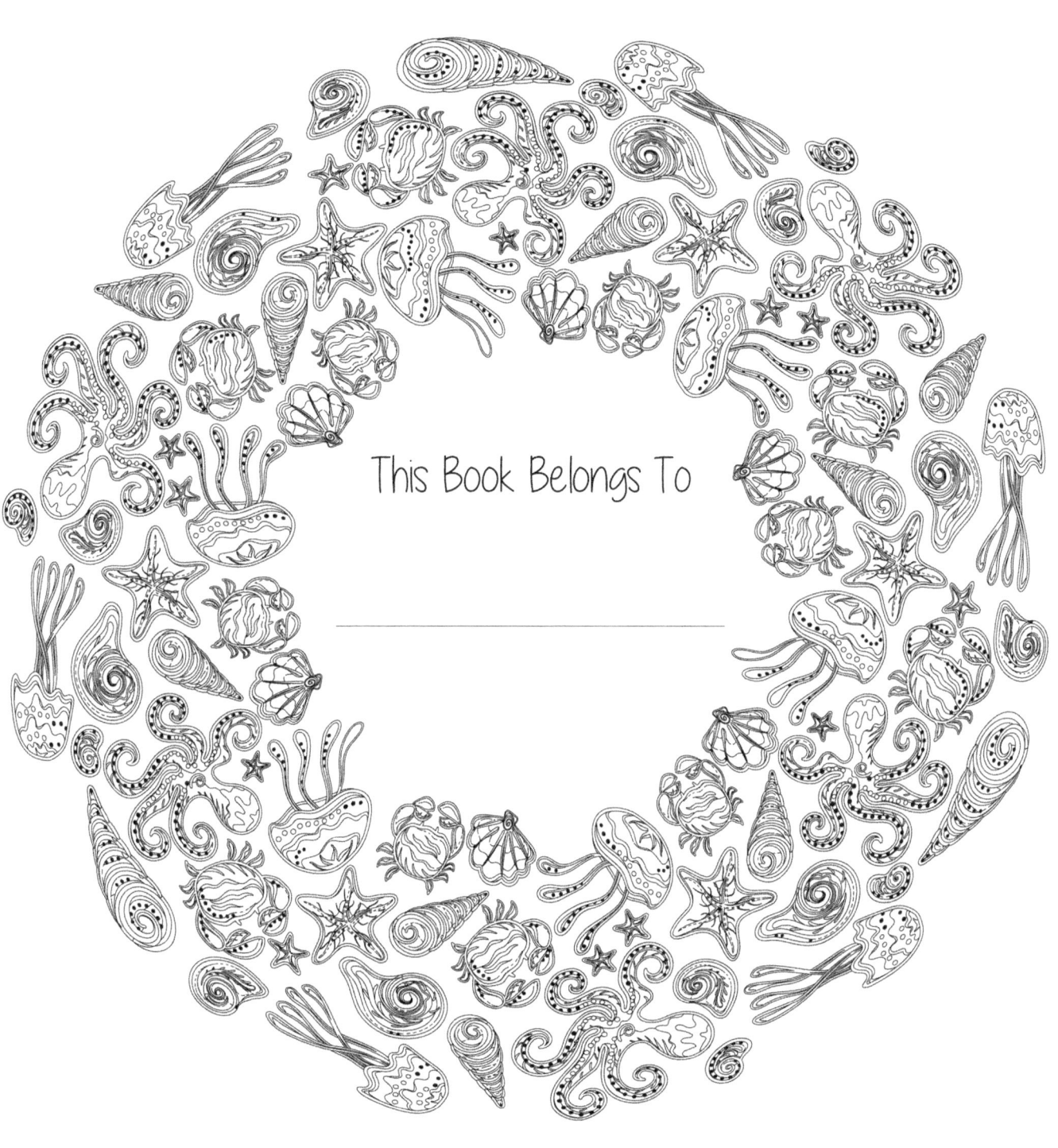

This Book Belongs To

_____

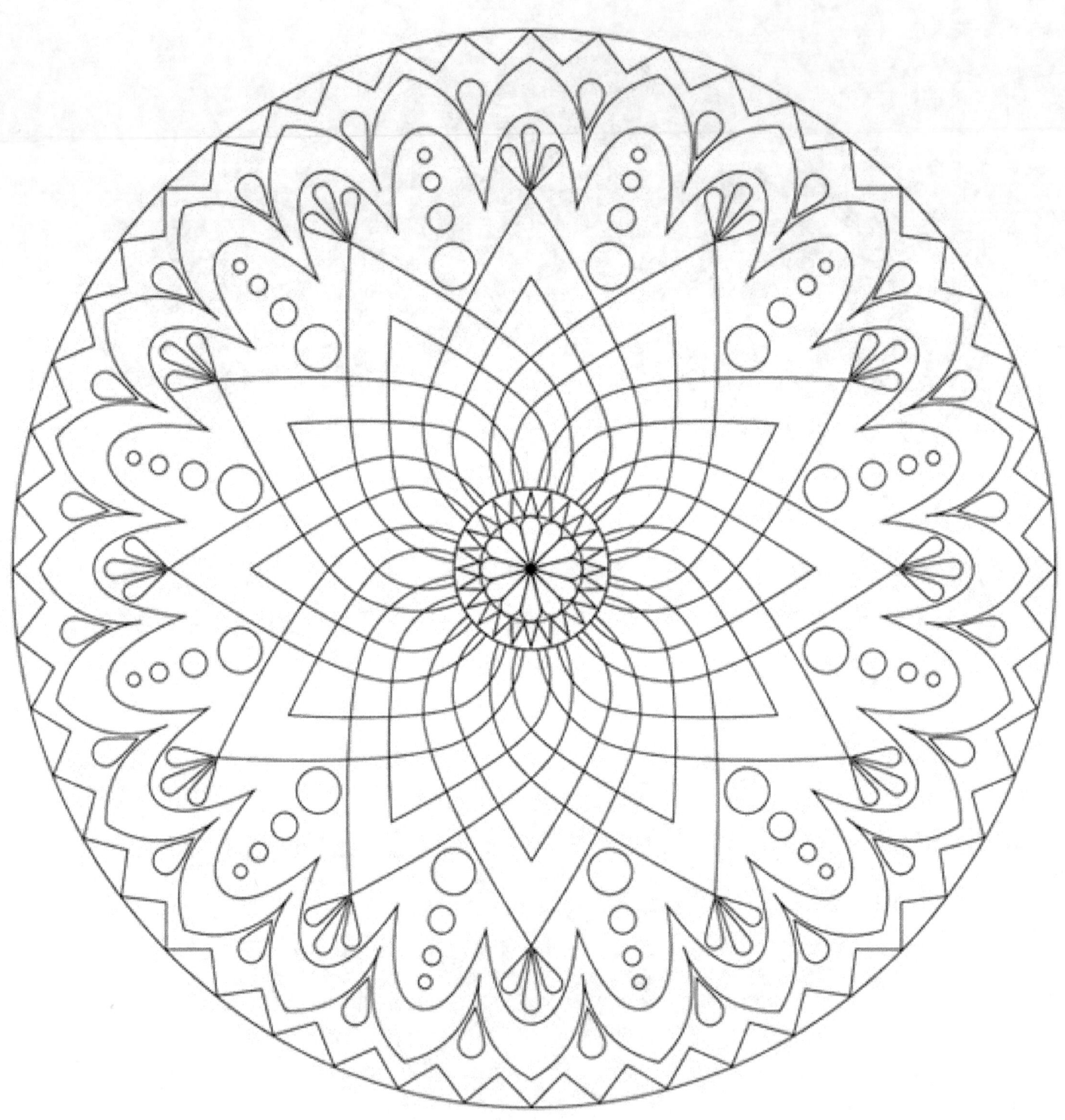

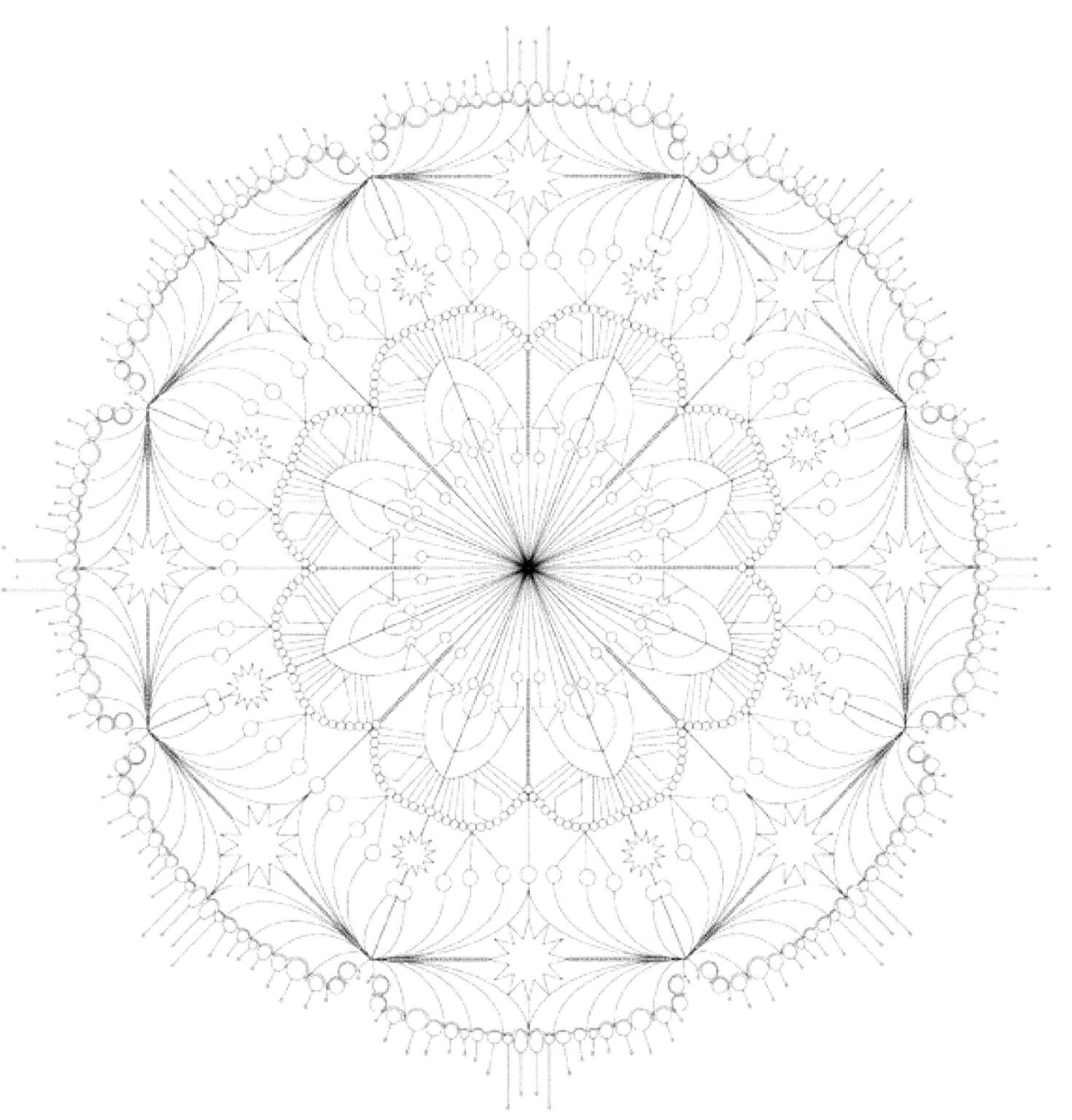

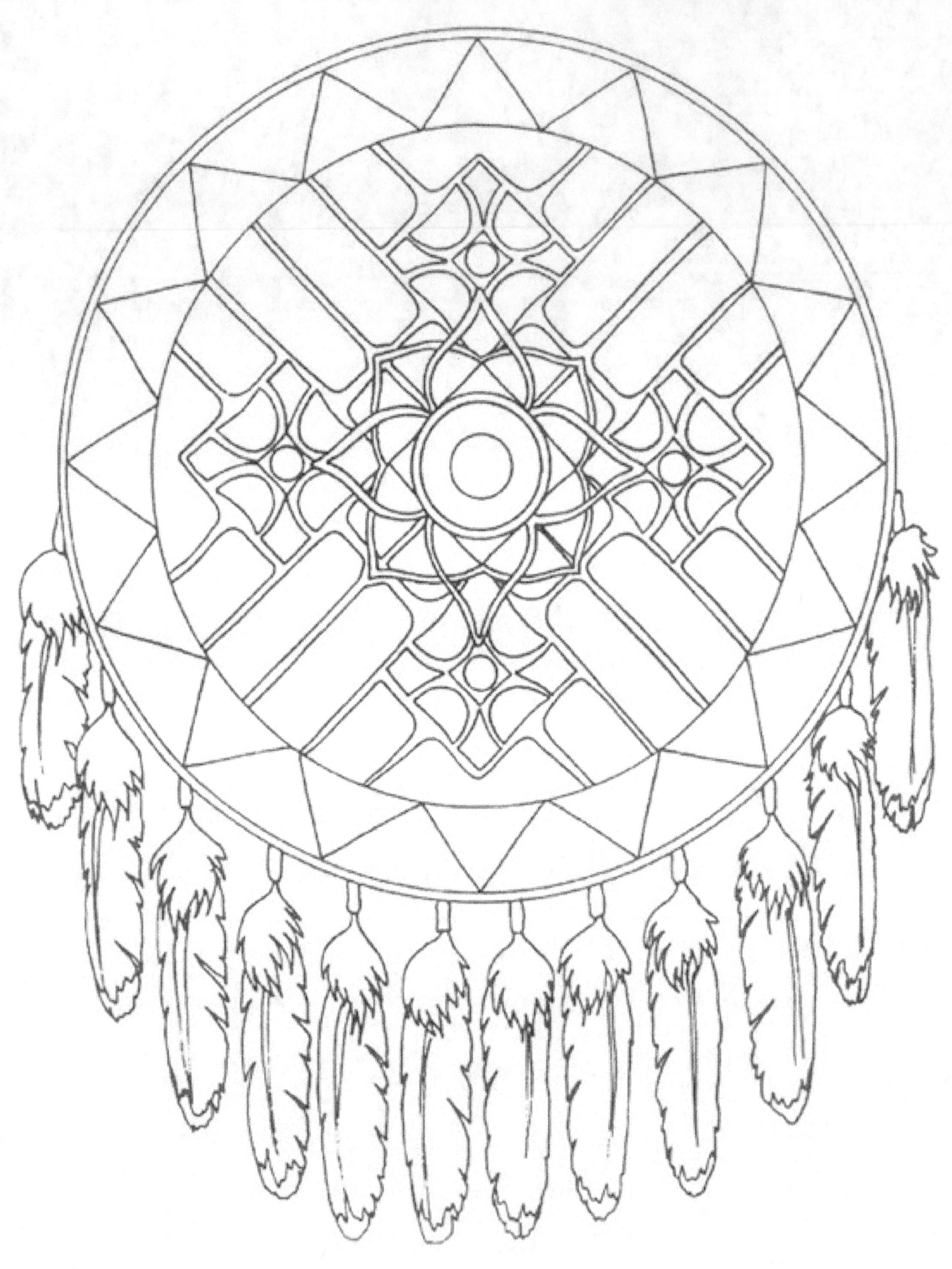

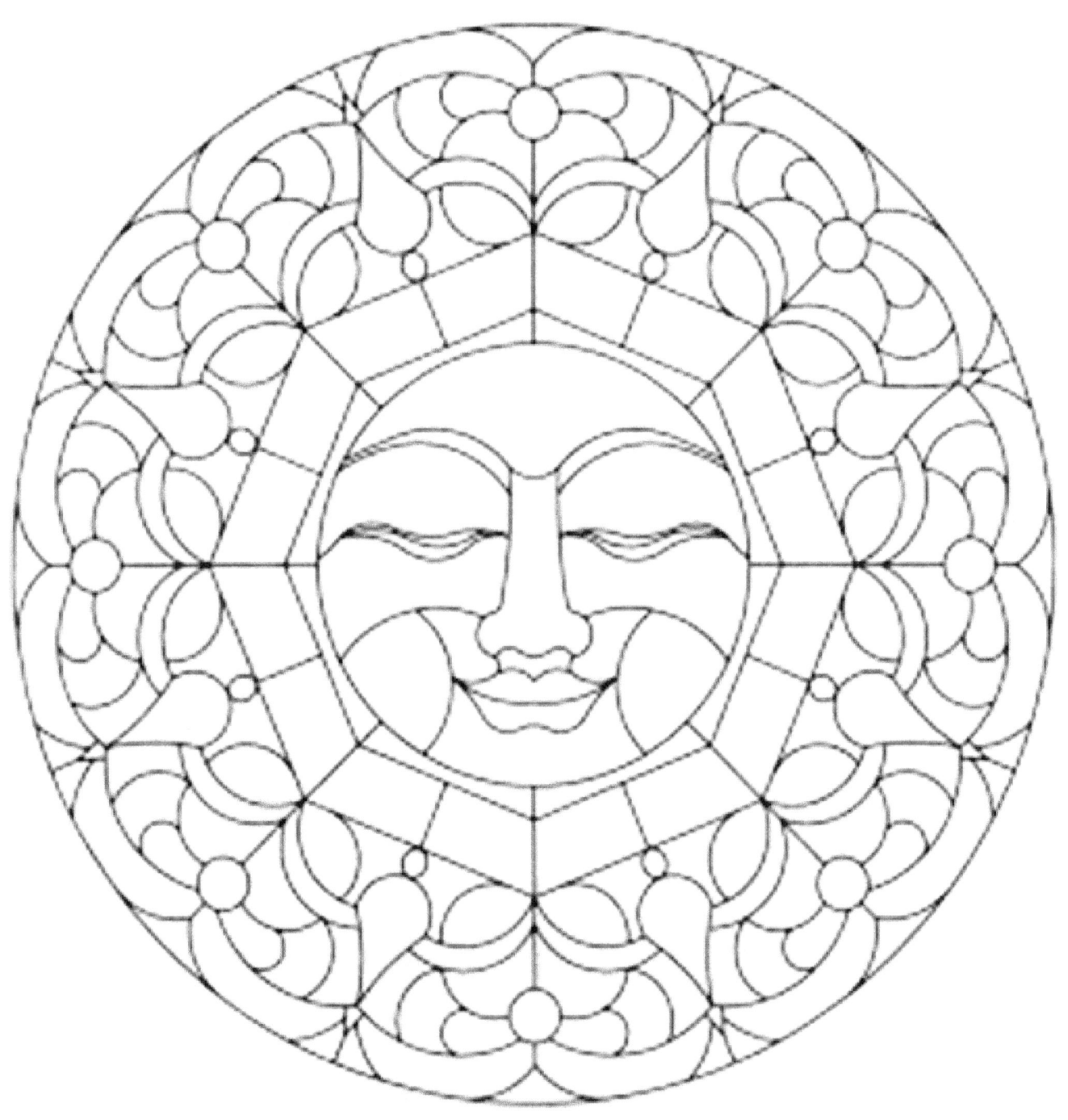

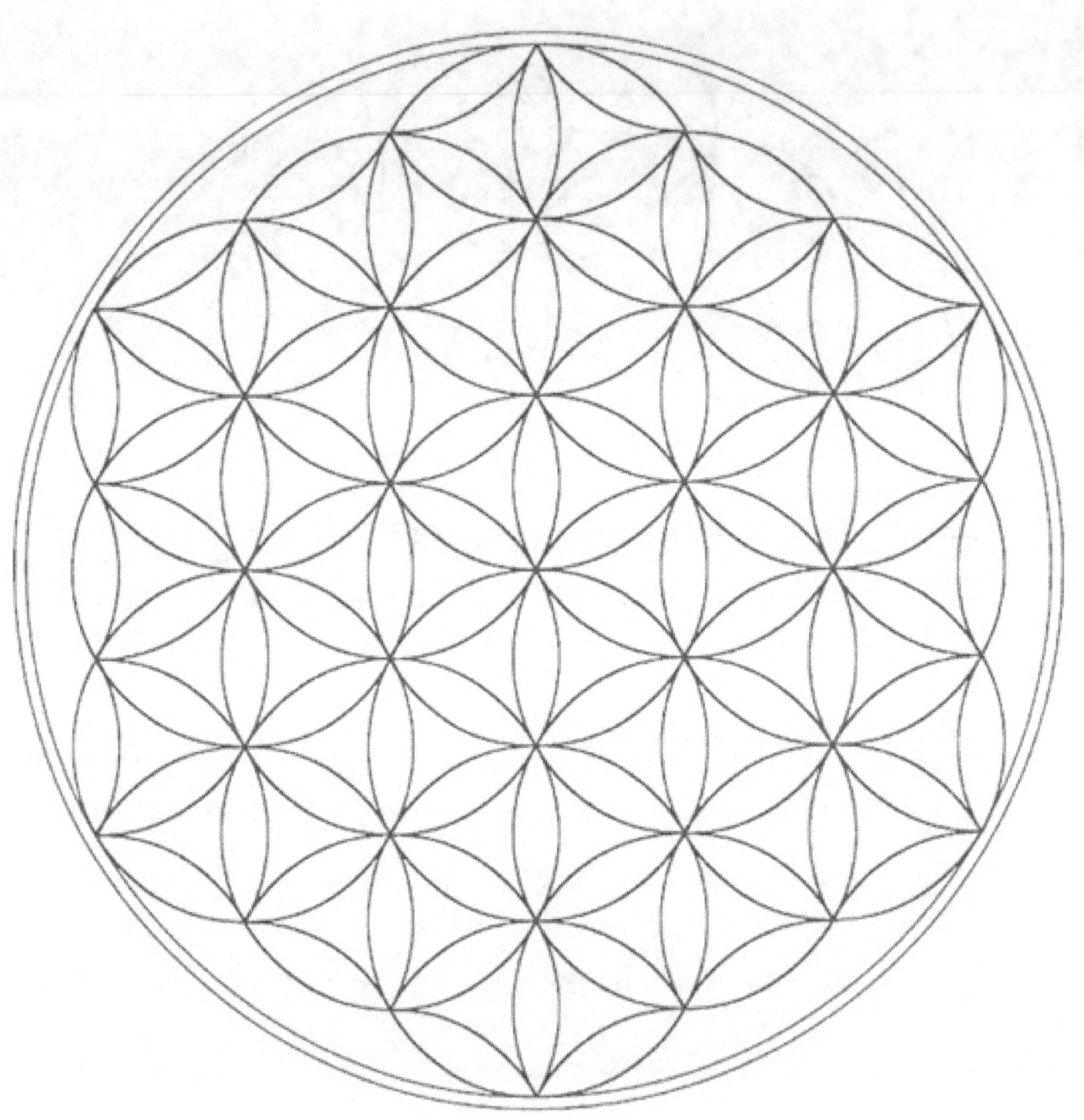

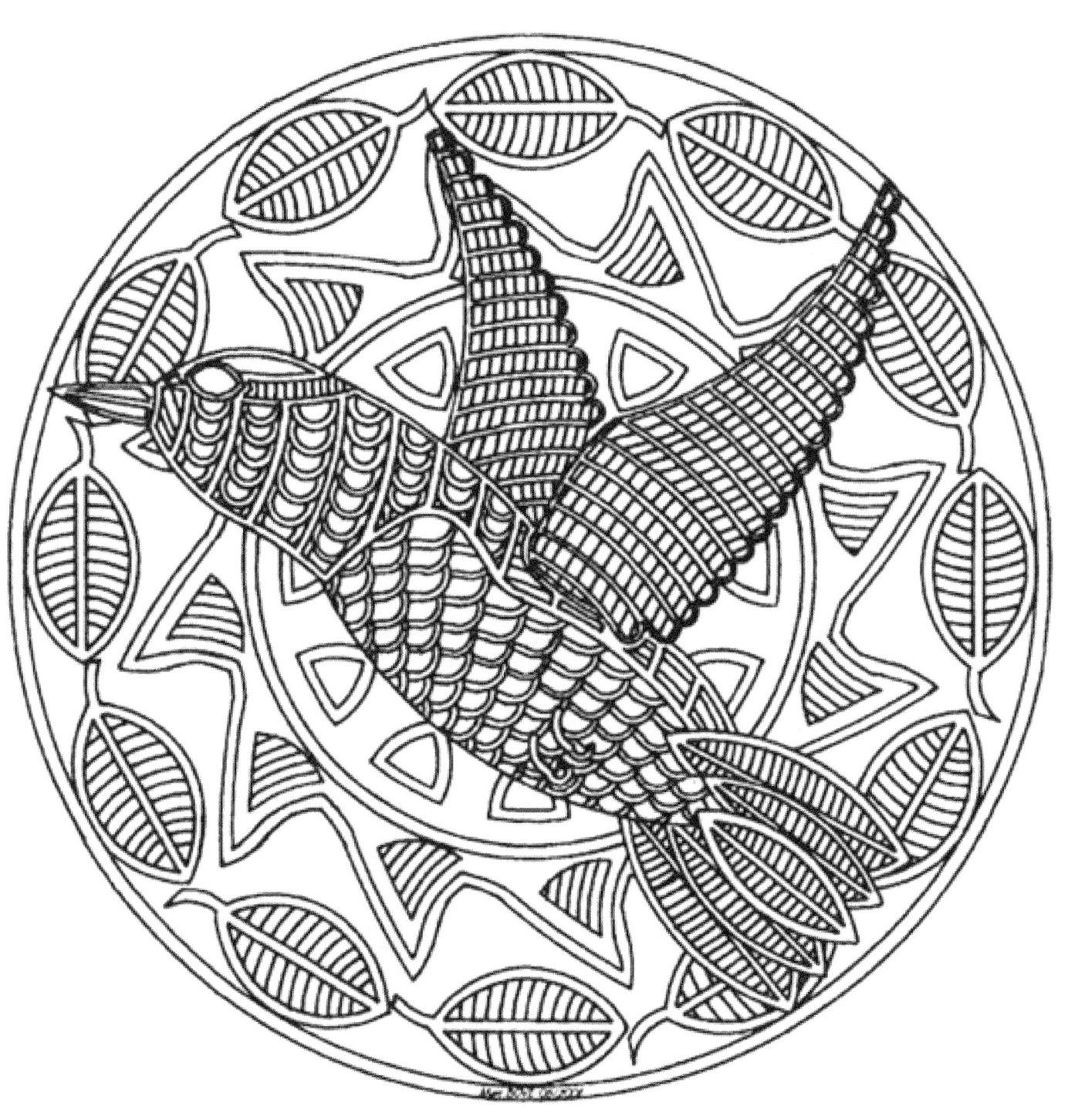

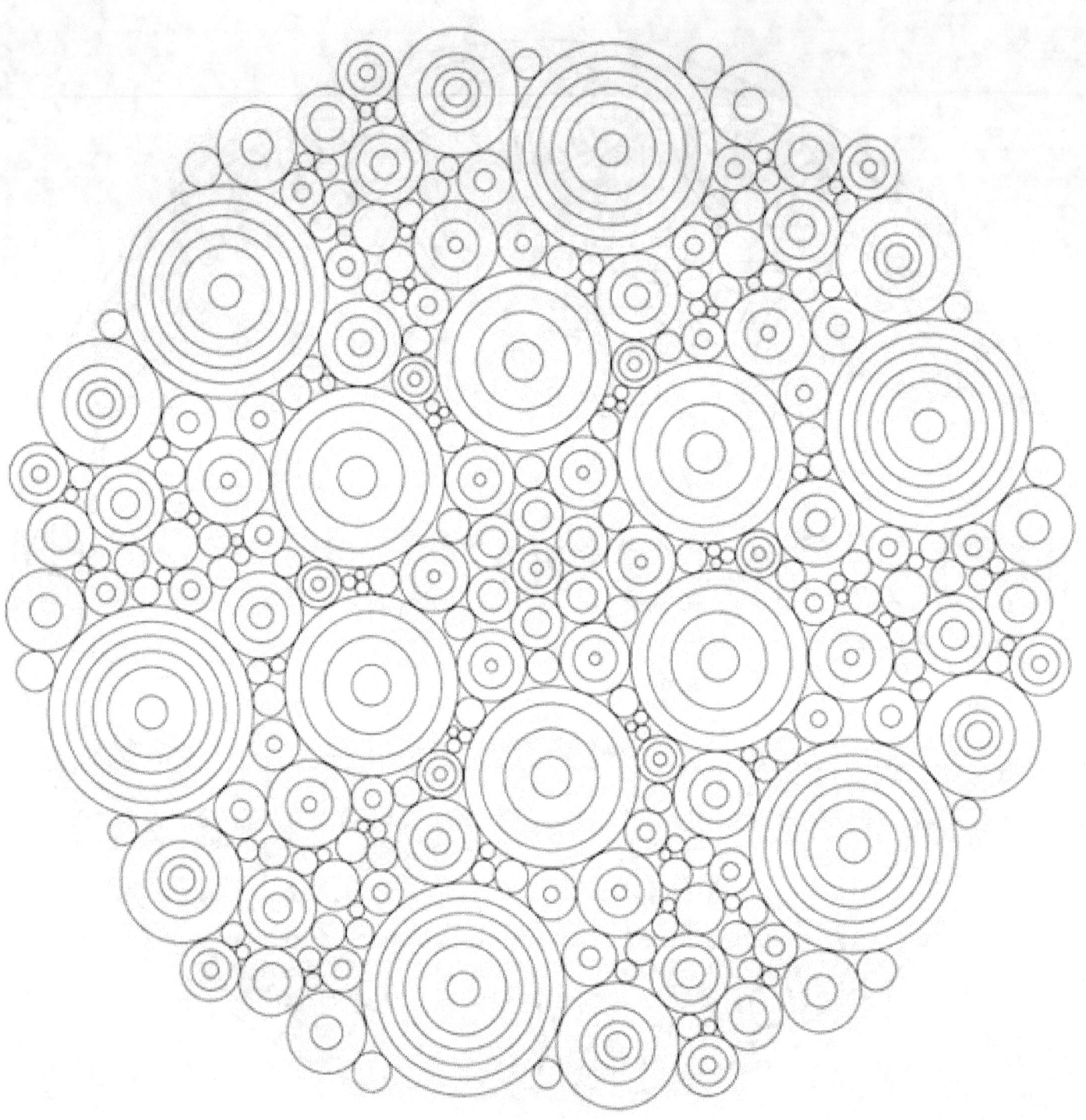

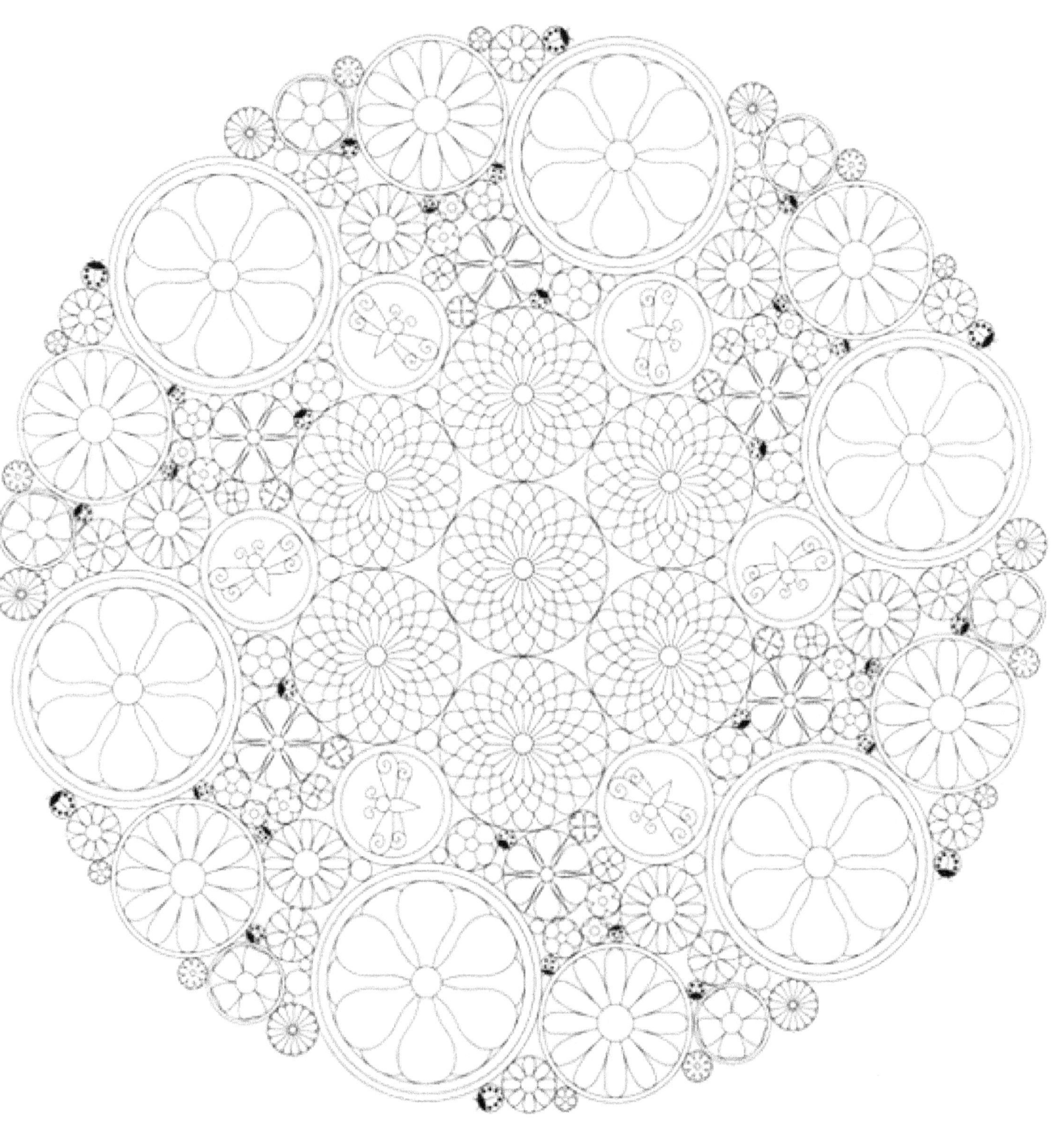

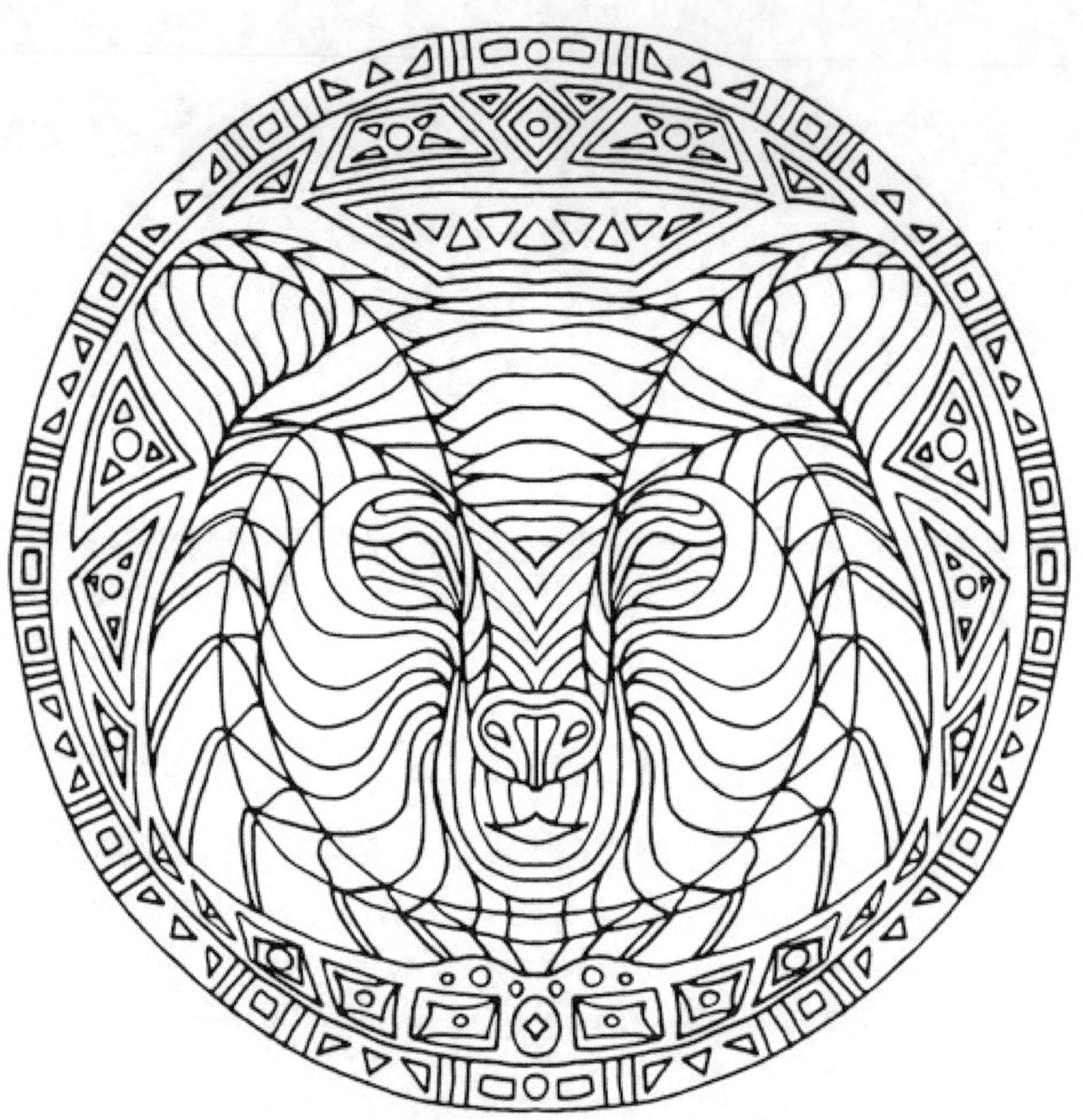

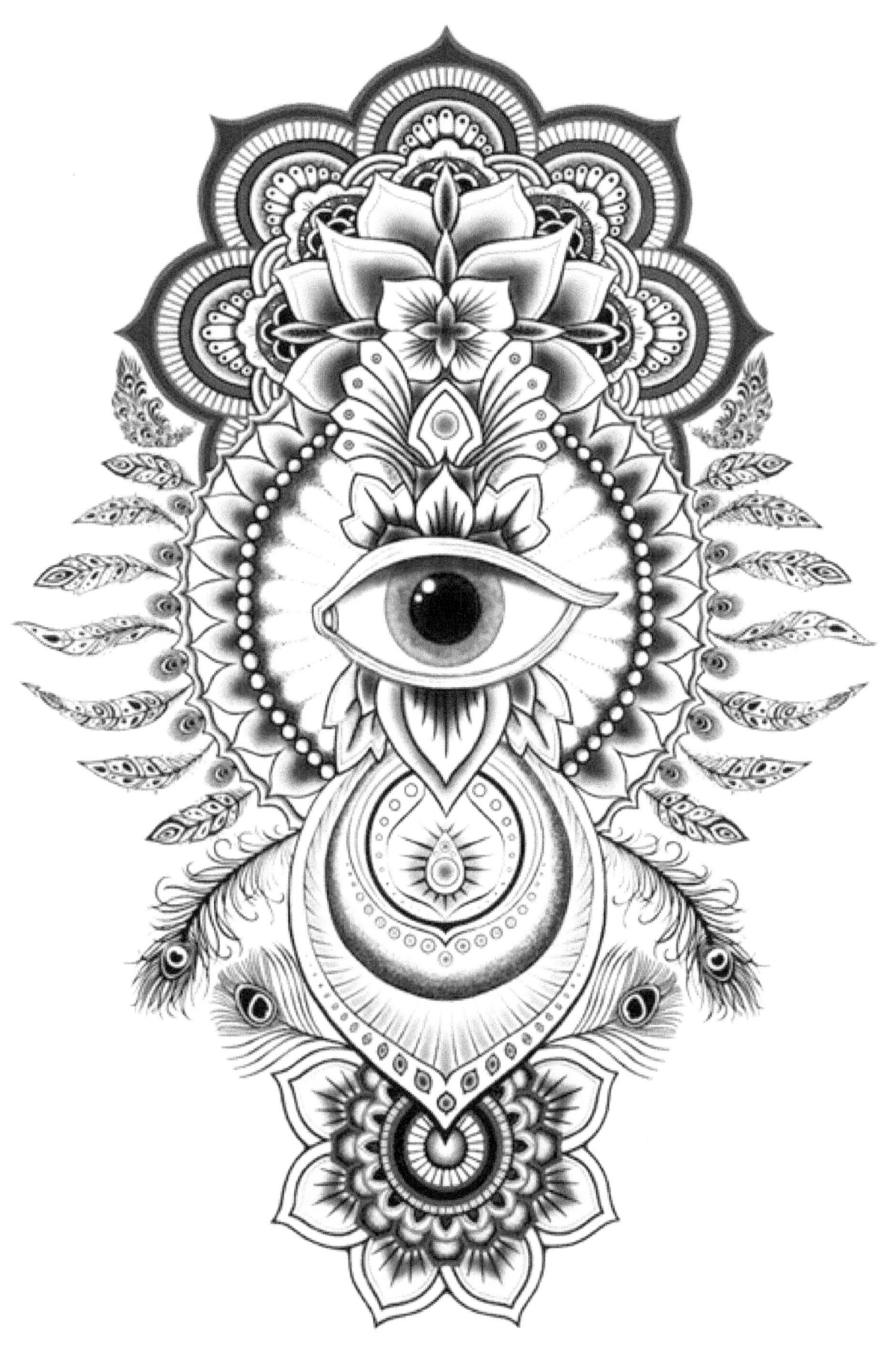

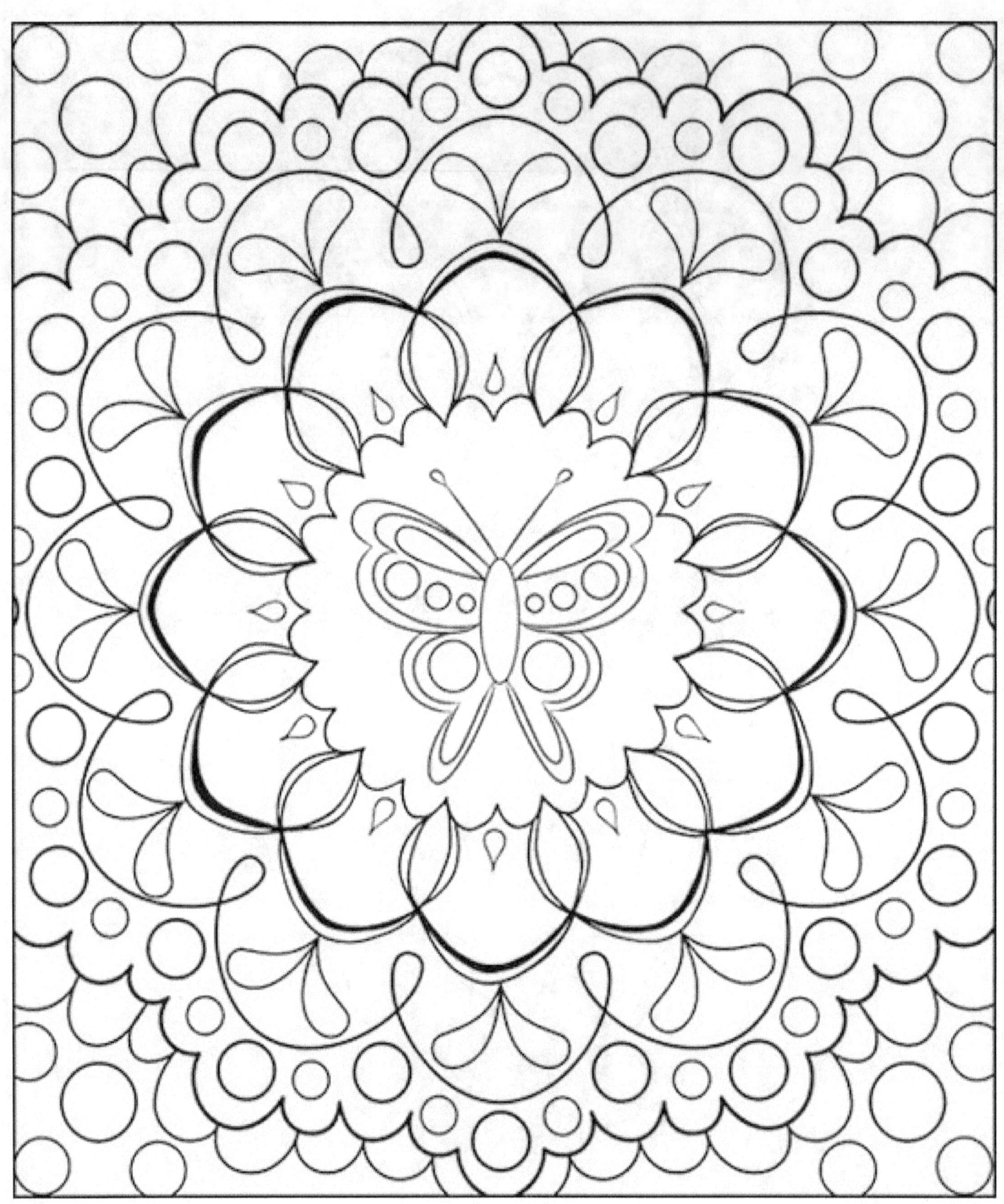

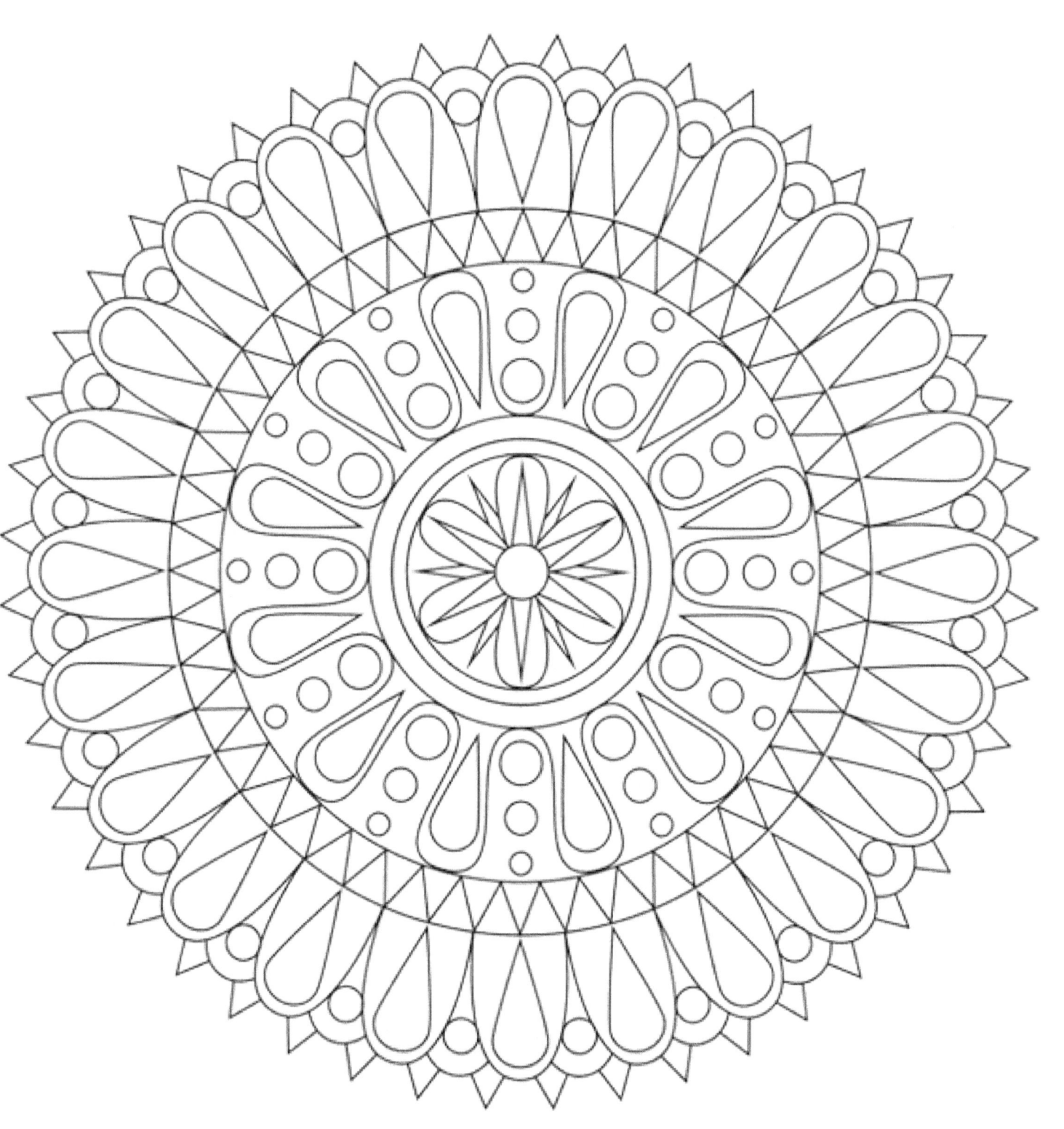

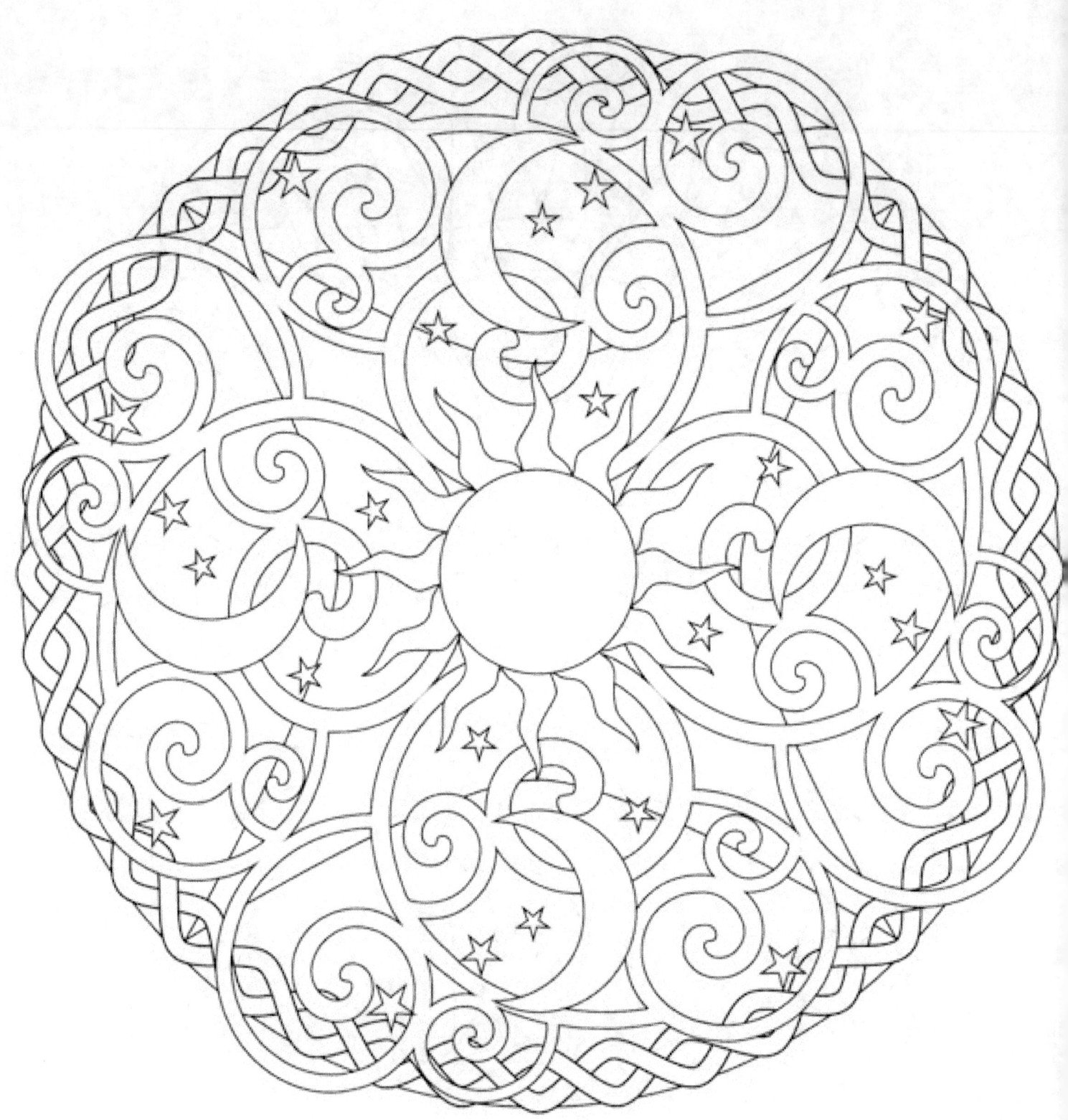

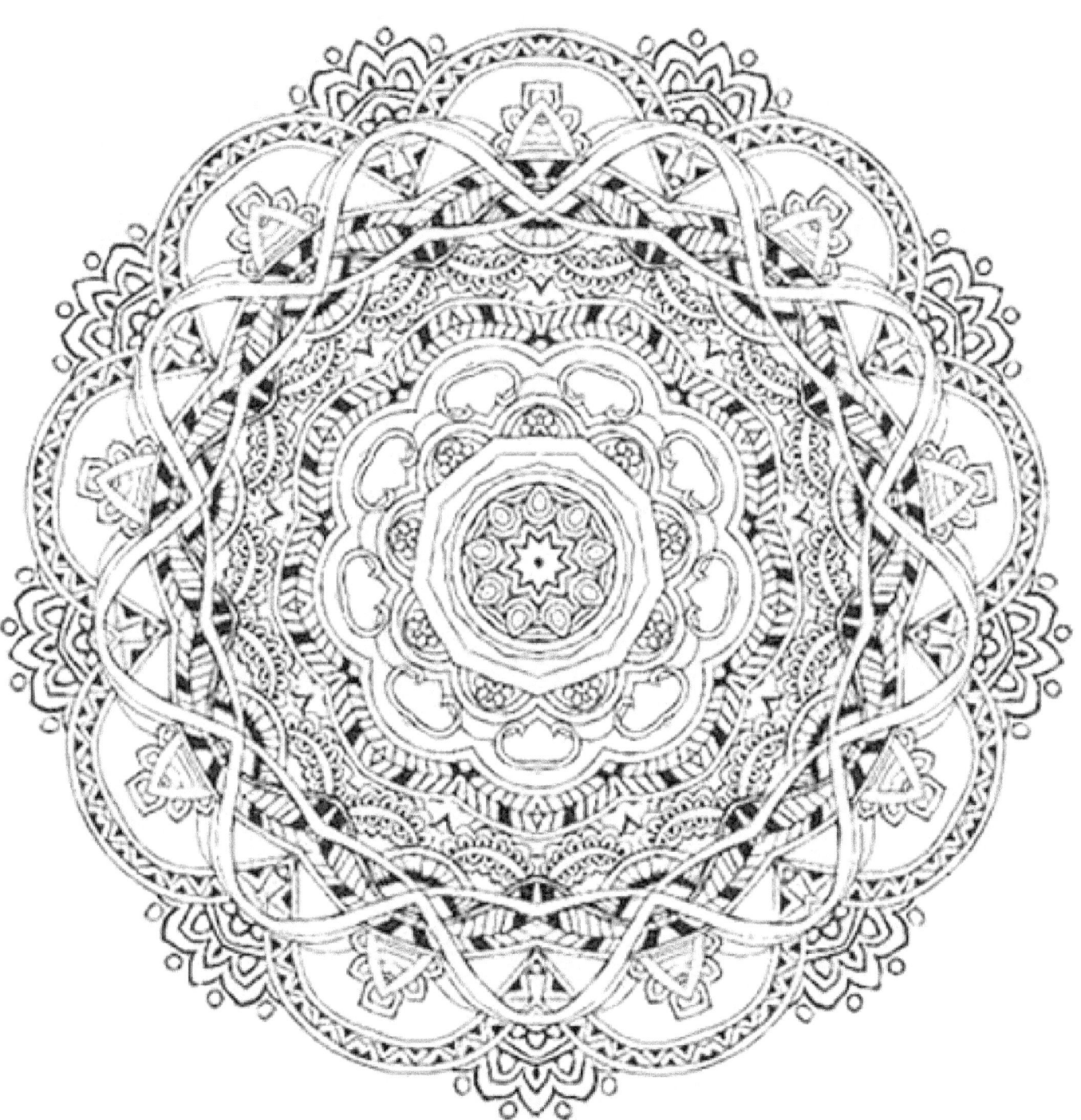

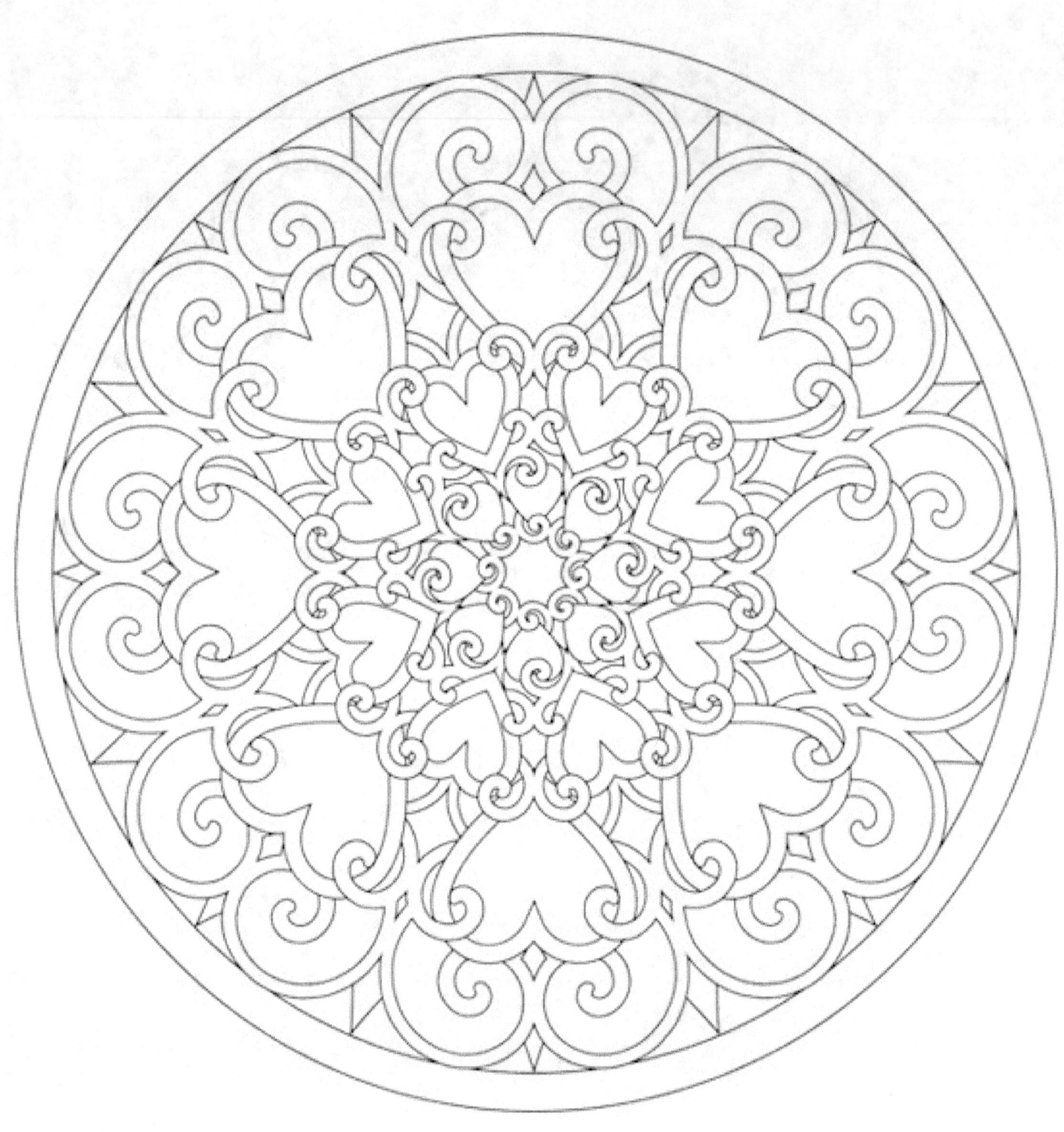

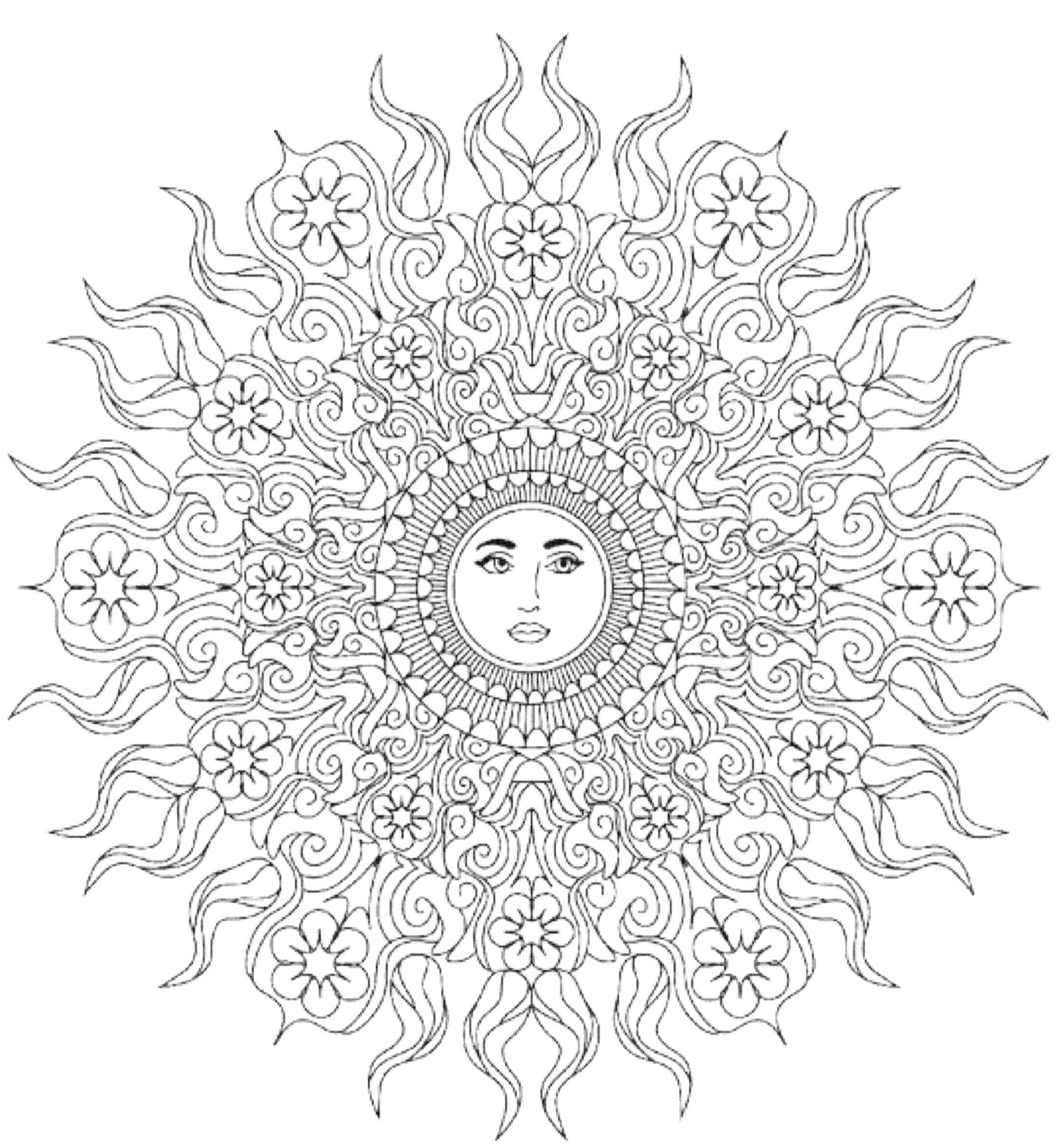

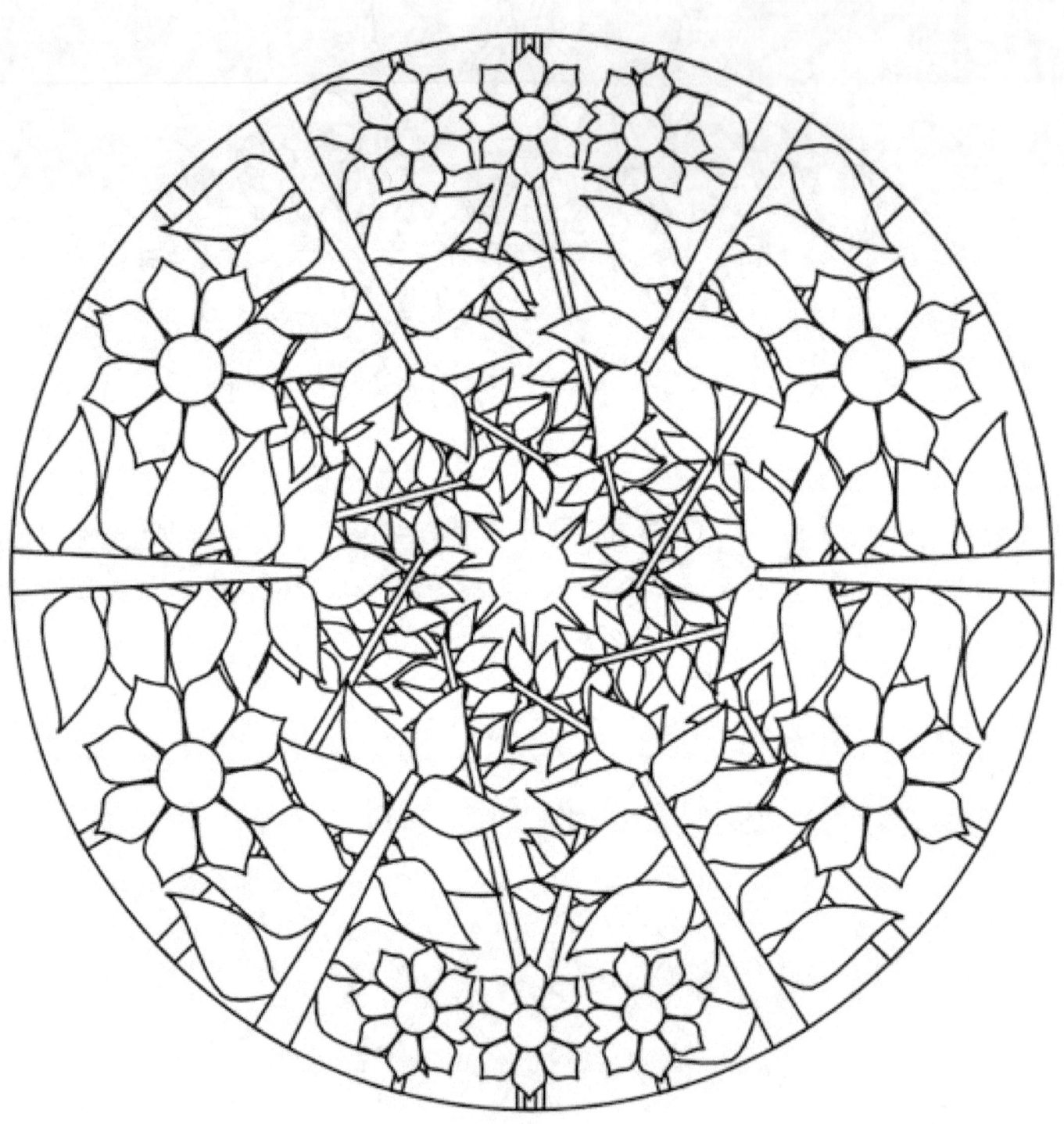

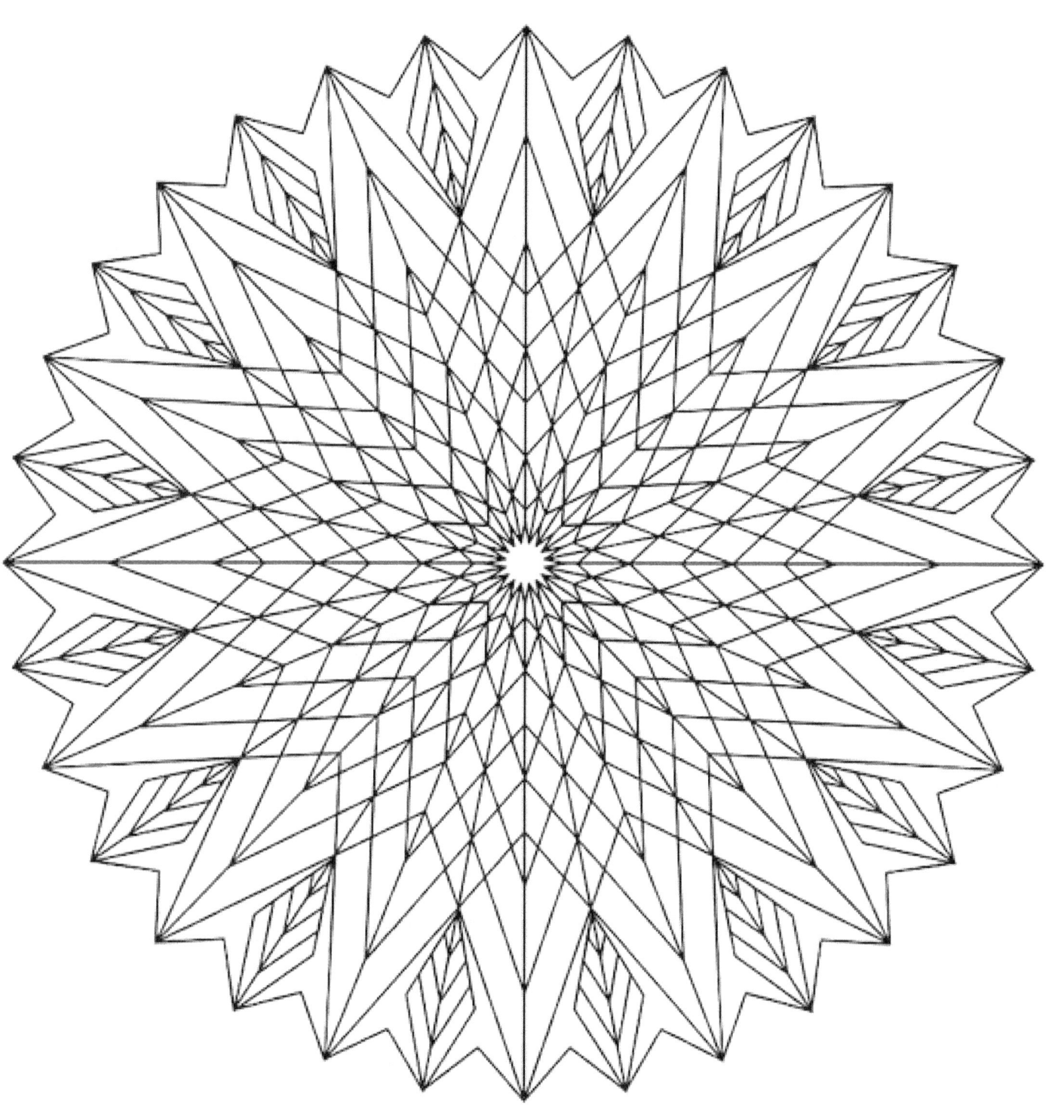

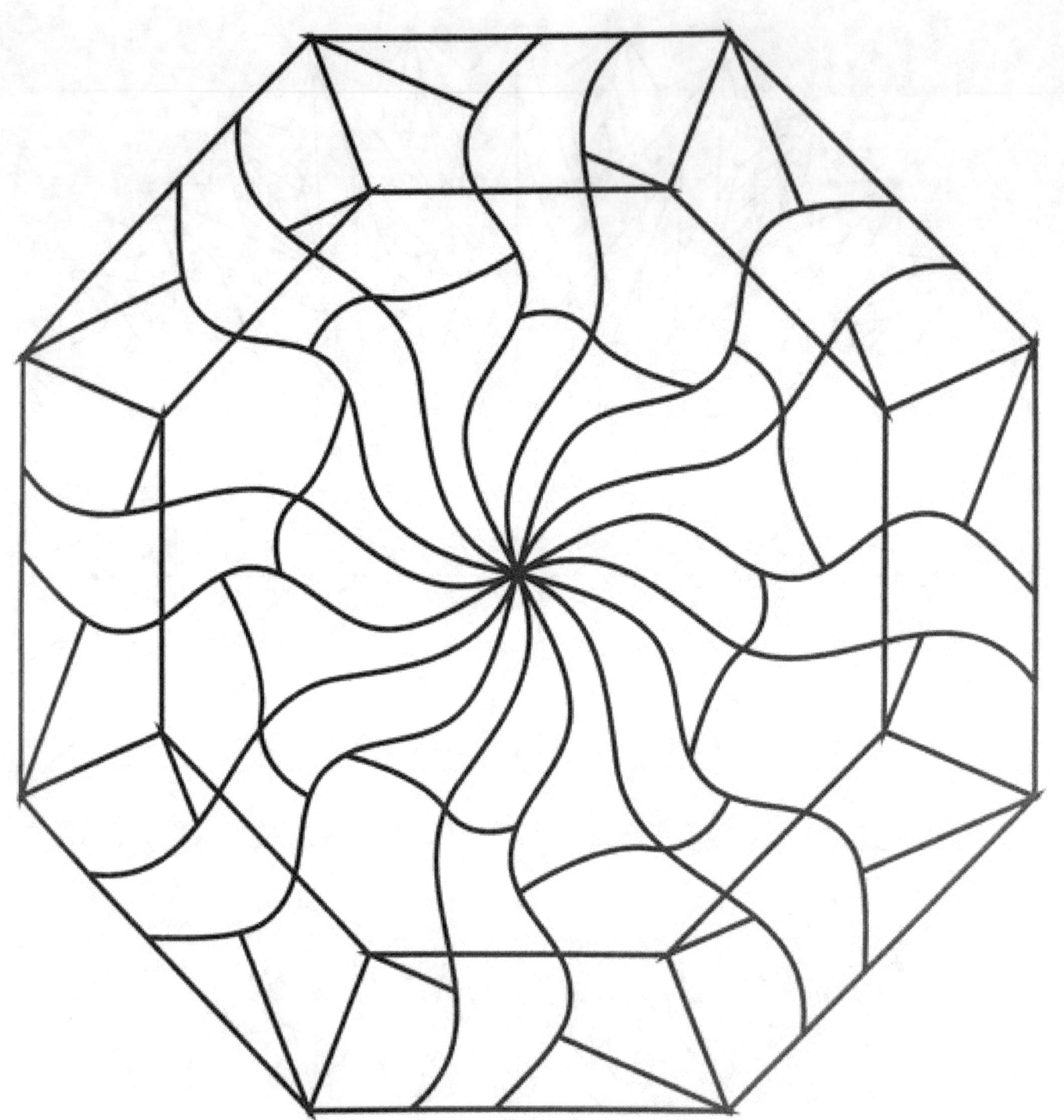

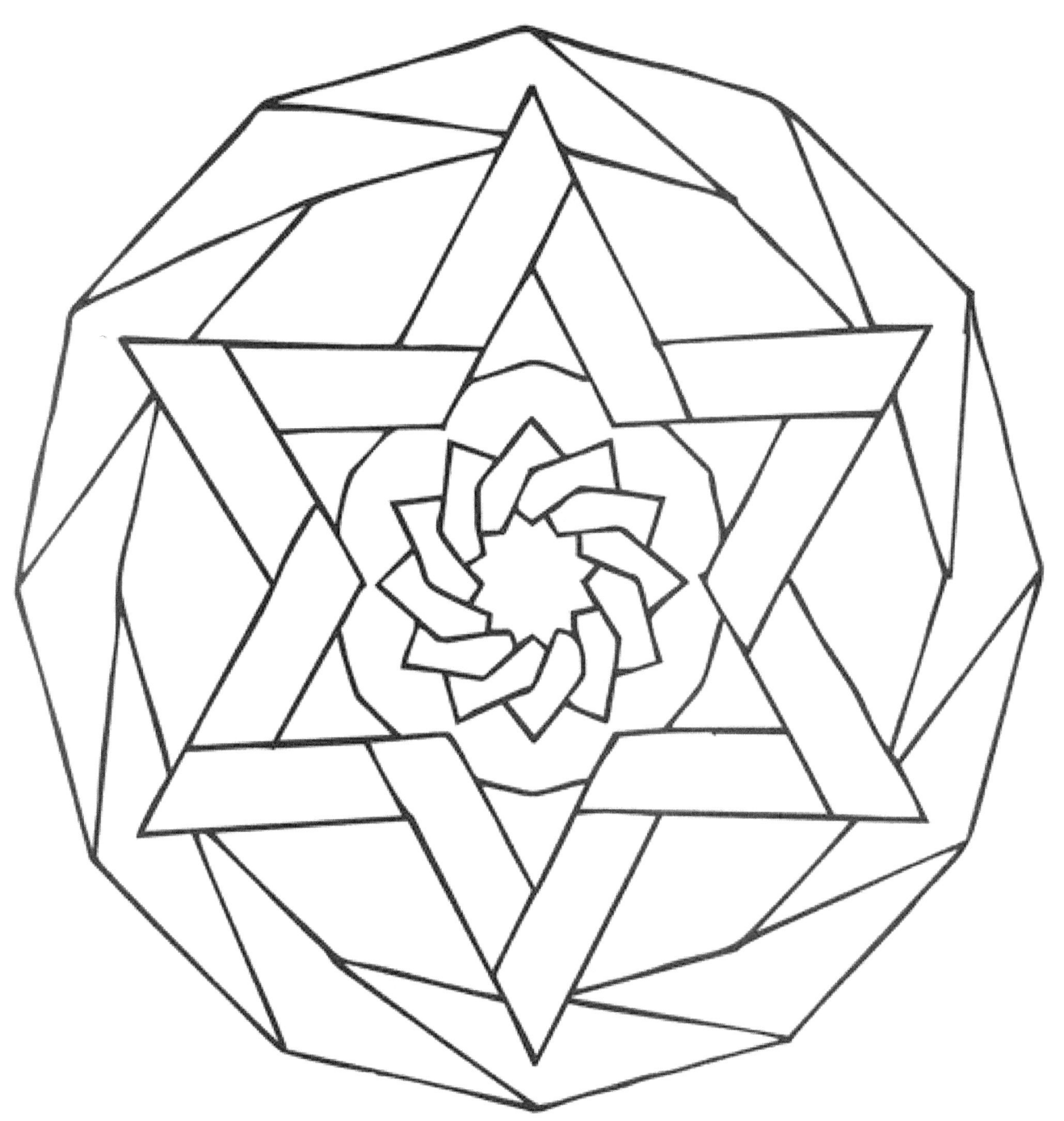

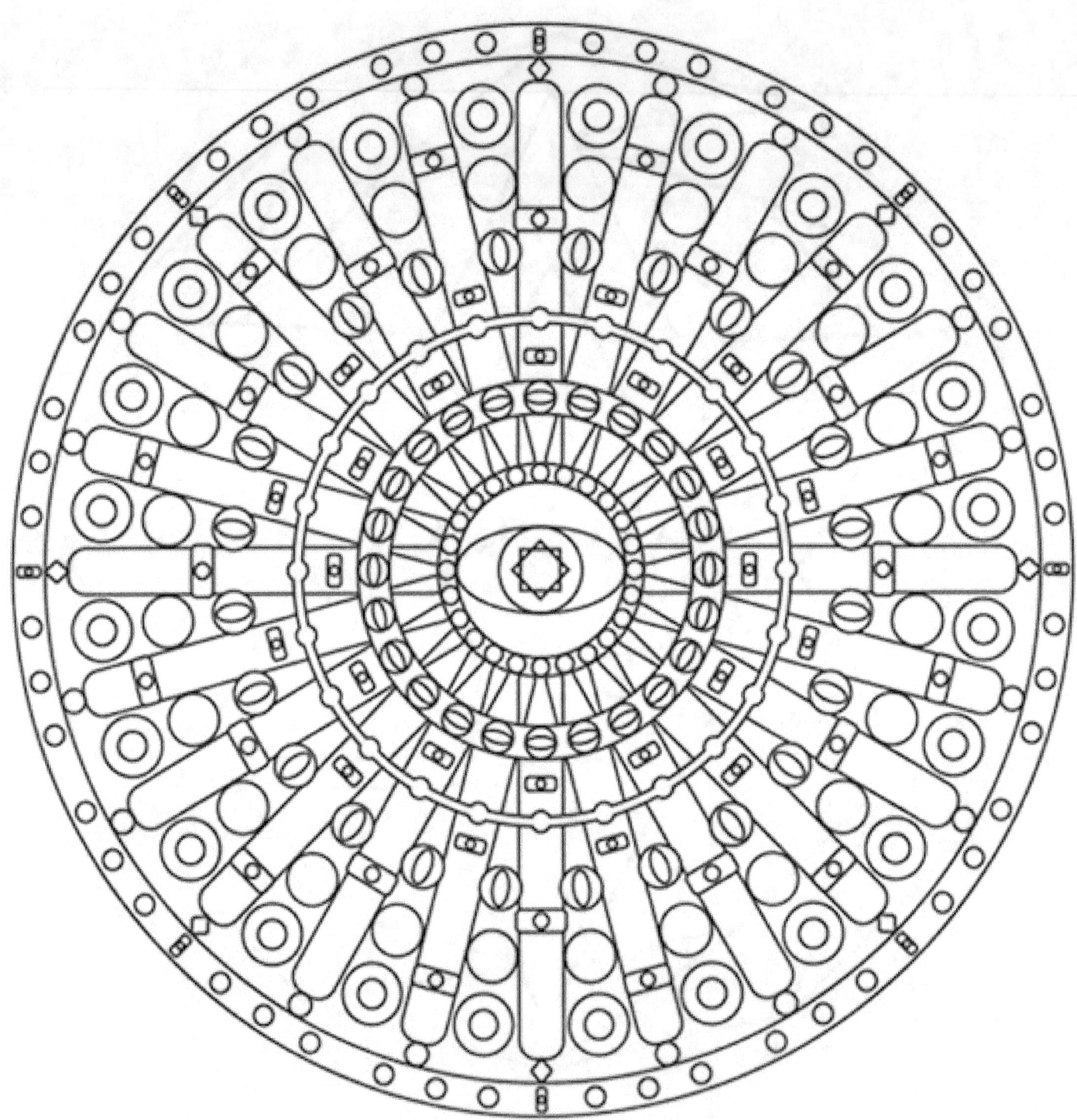

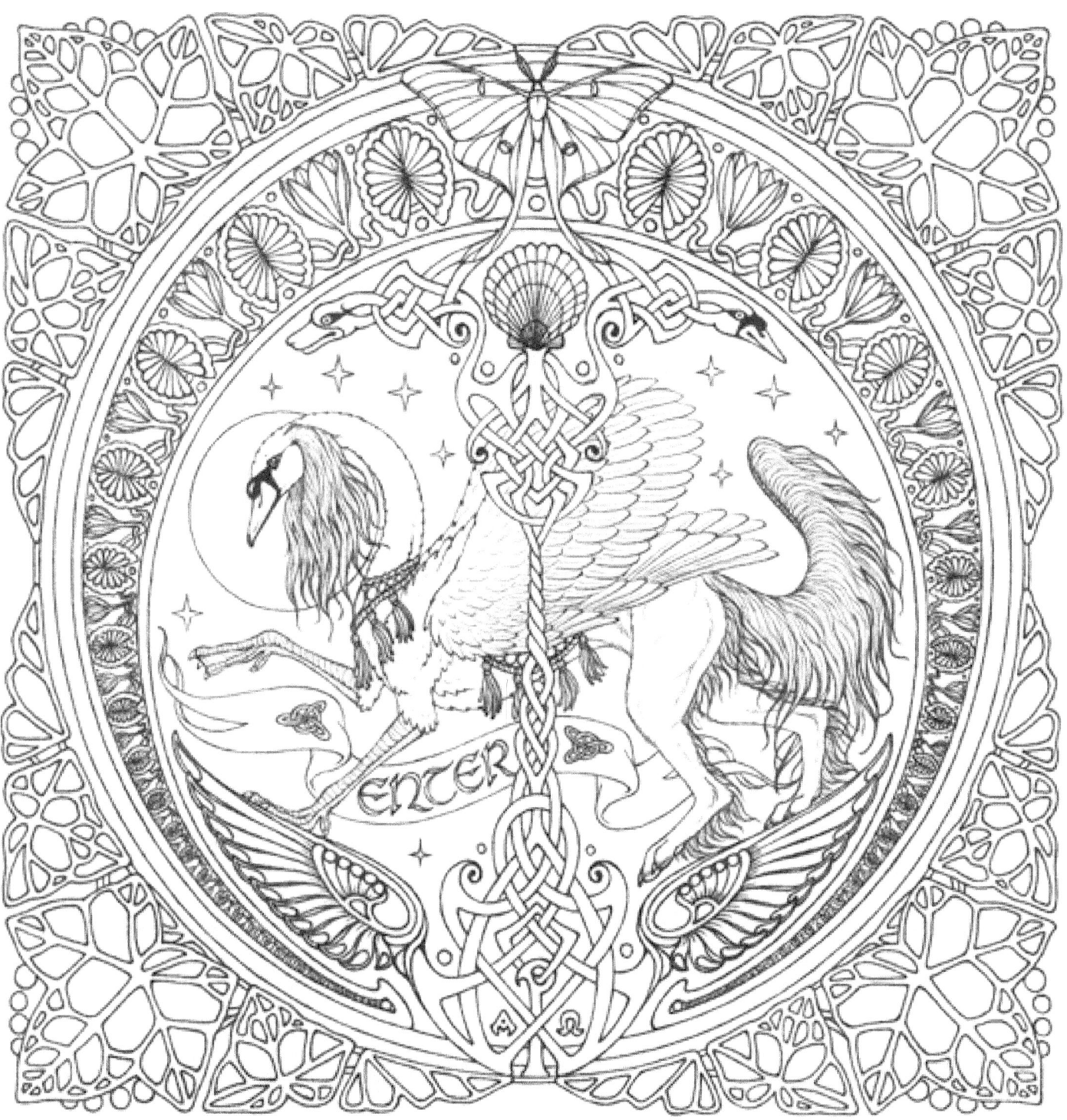

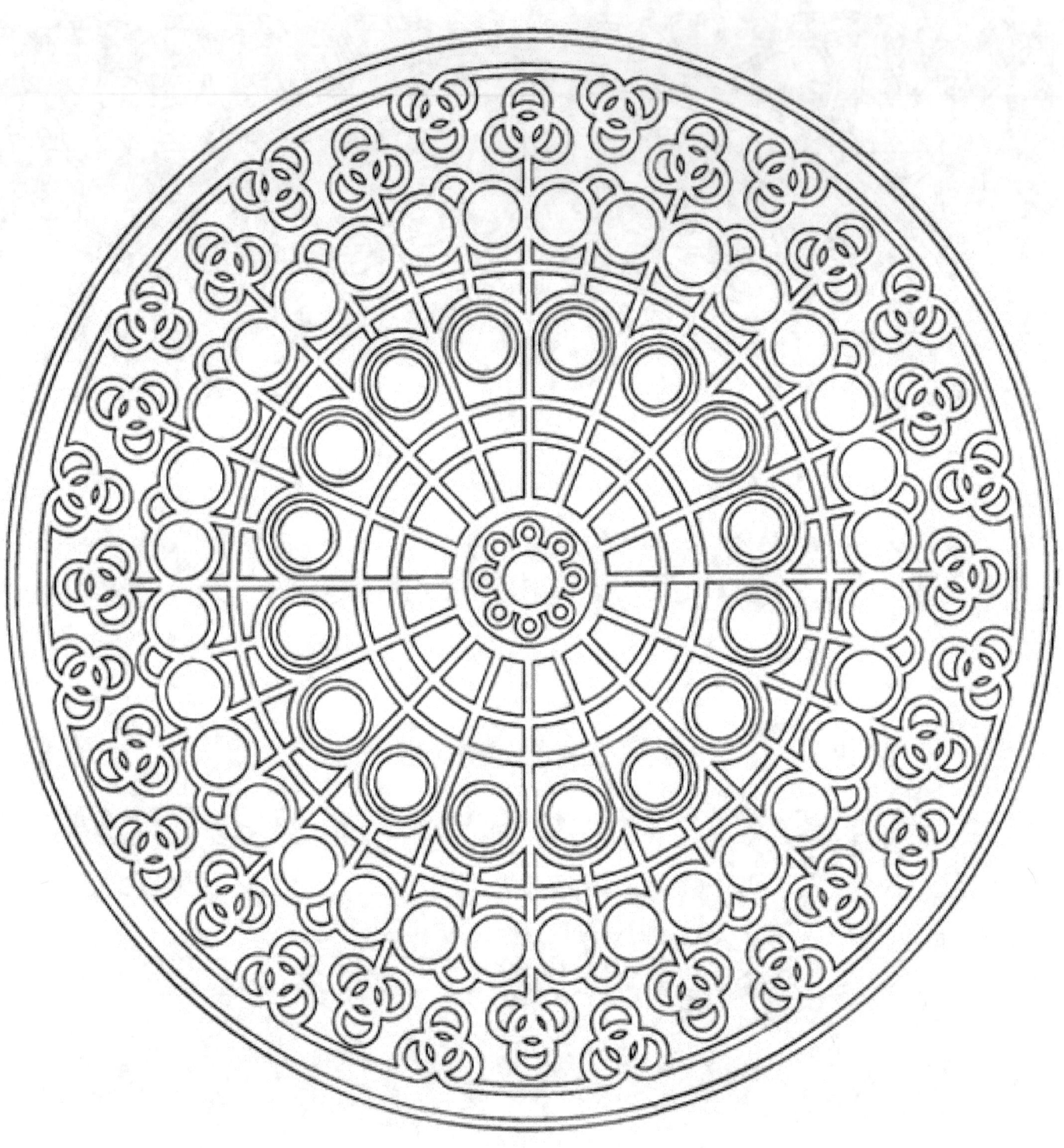

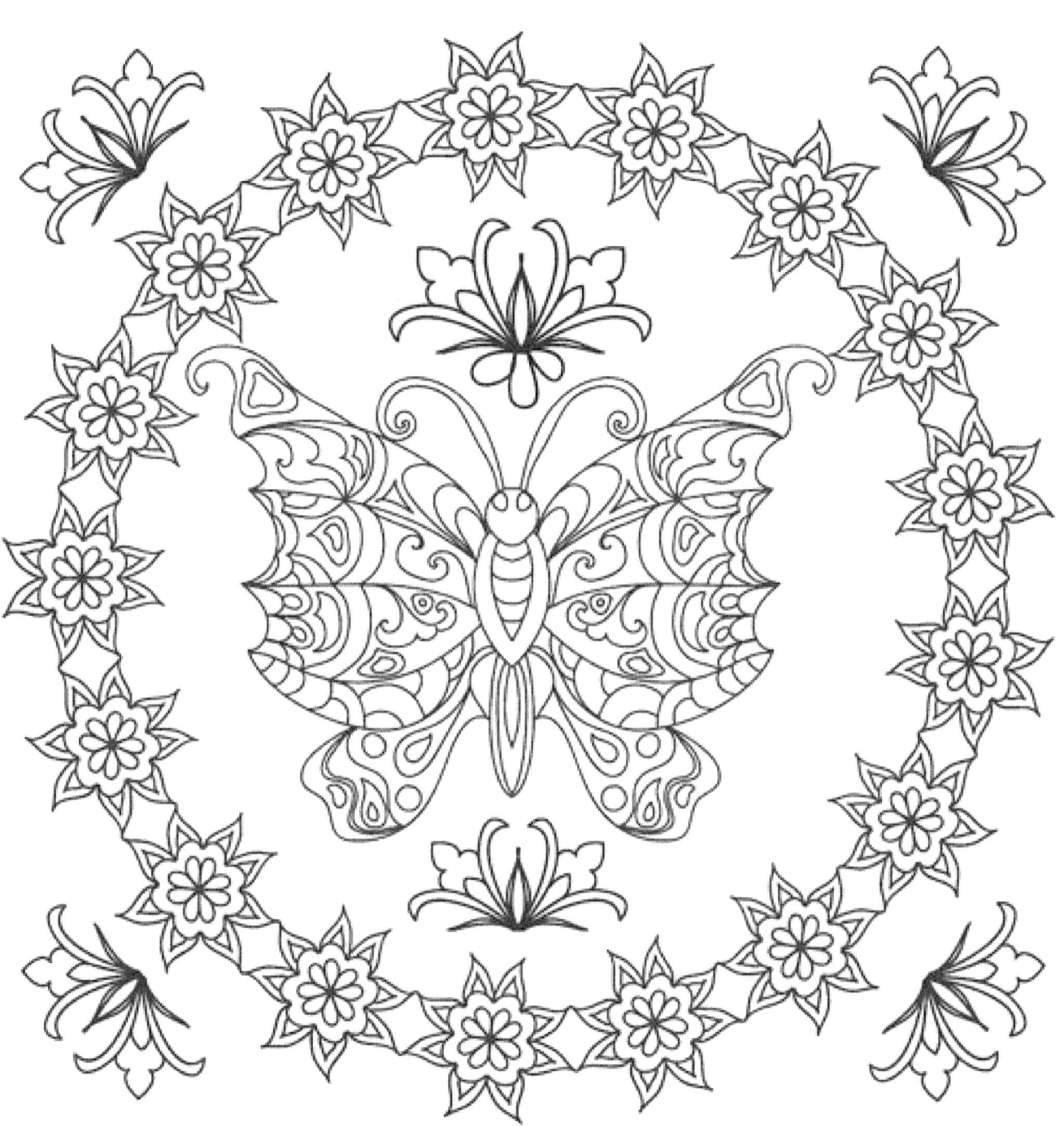

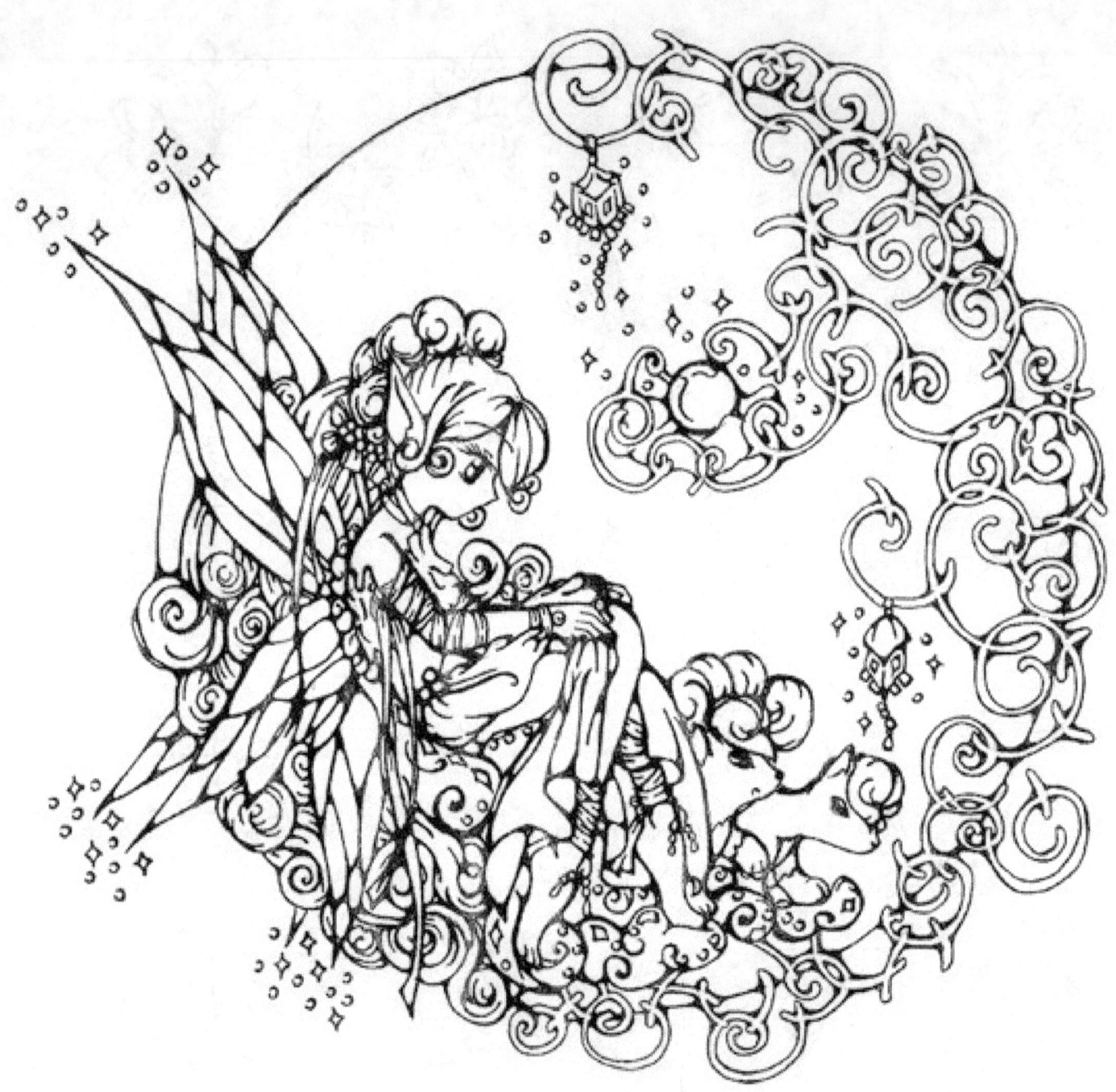

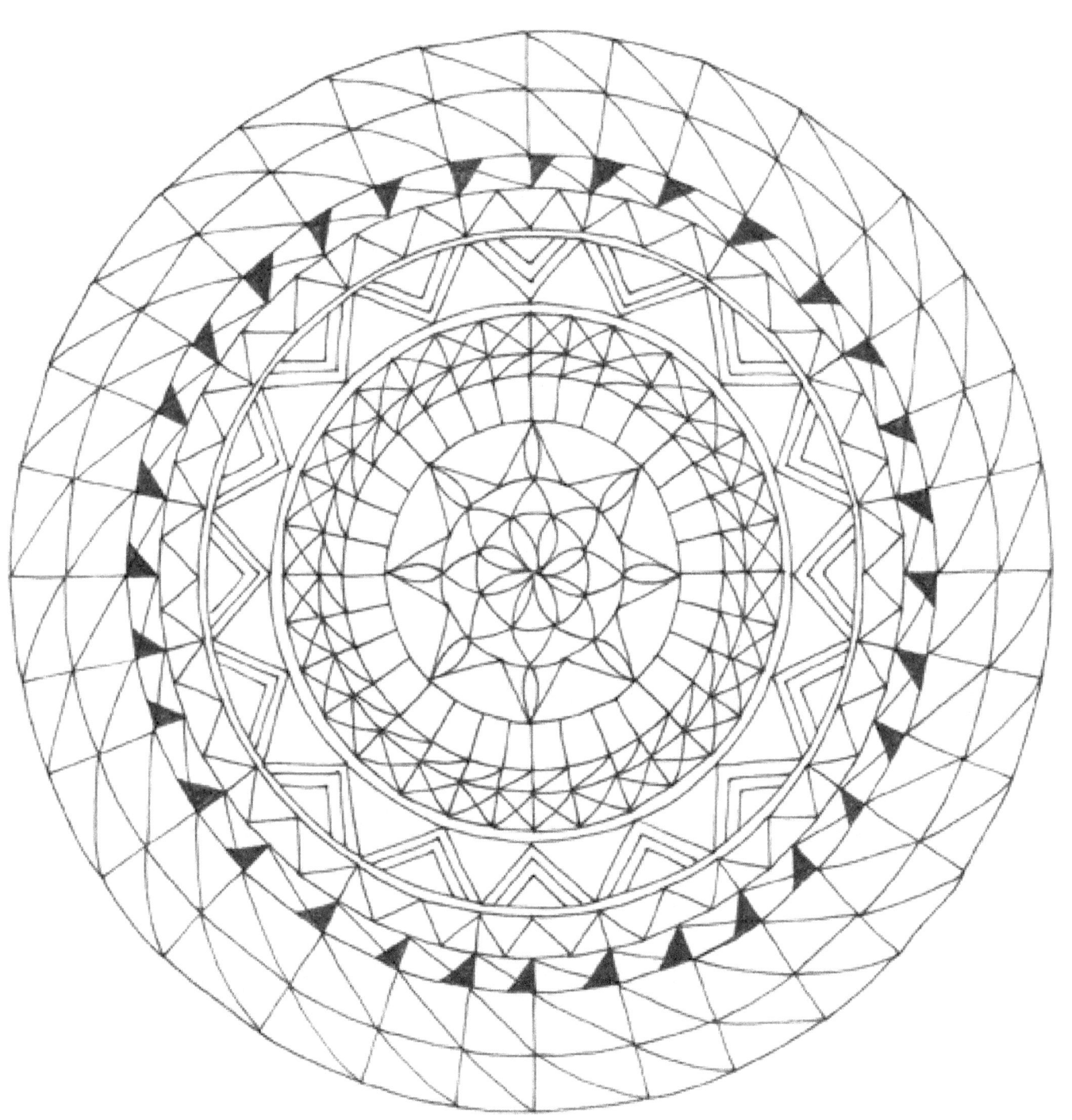

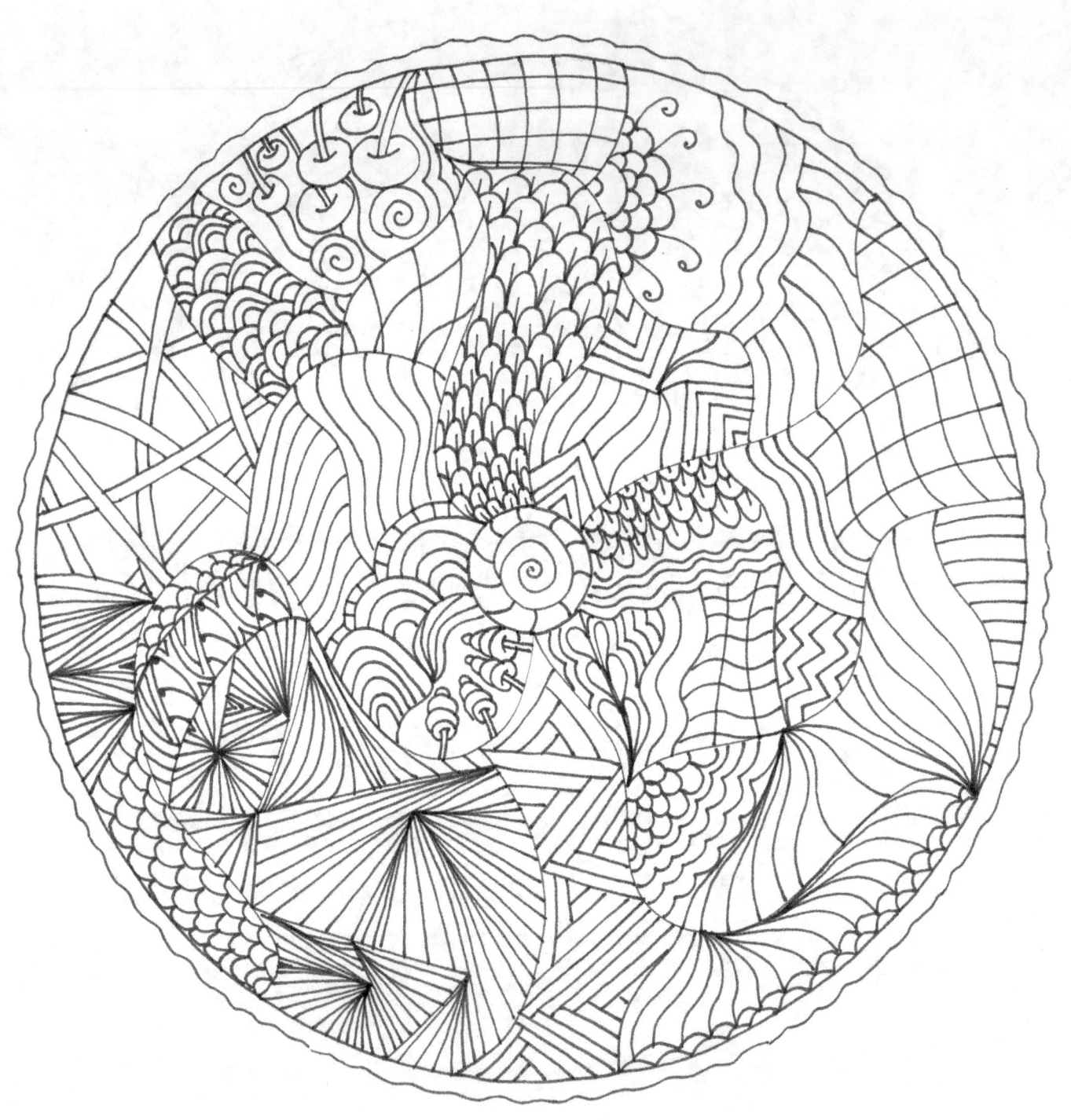

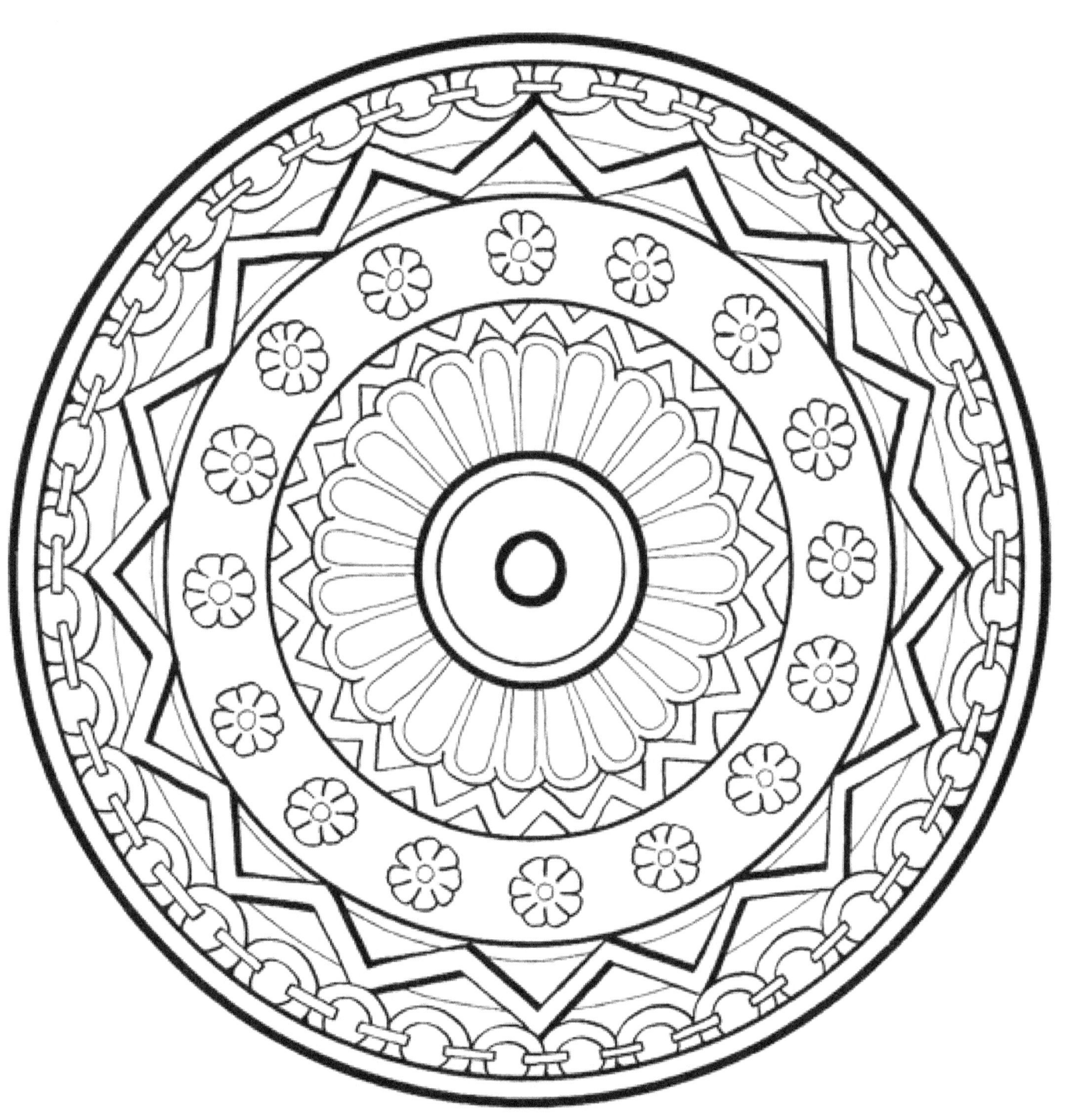

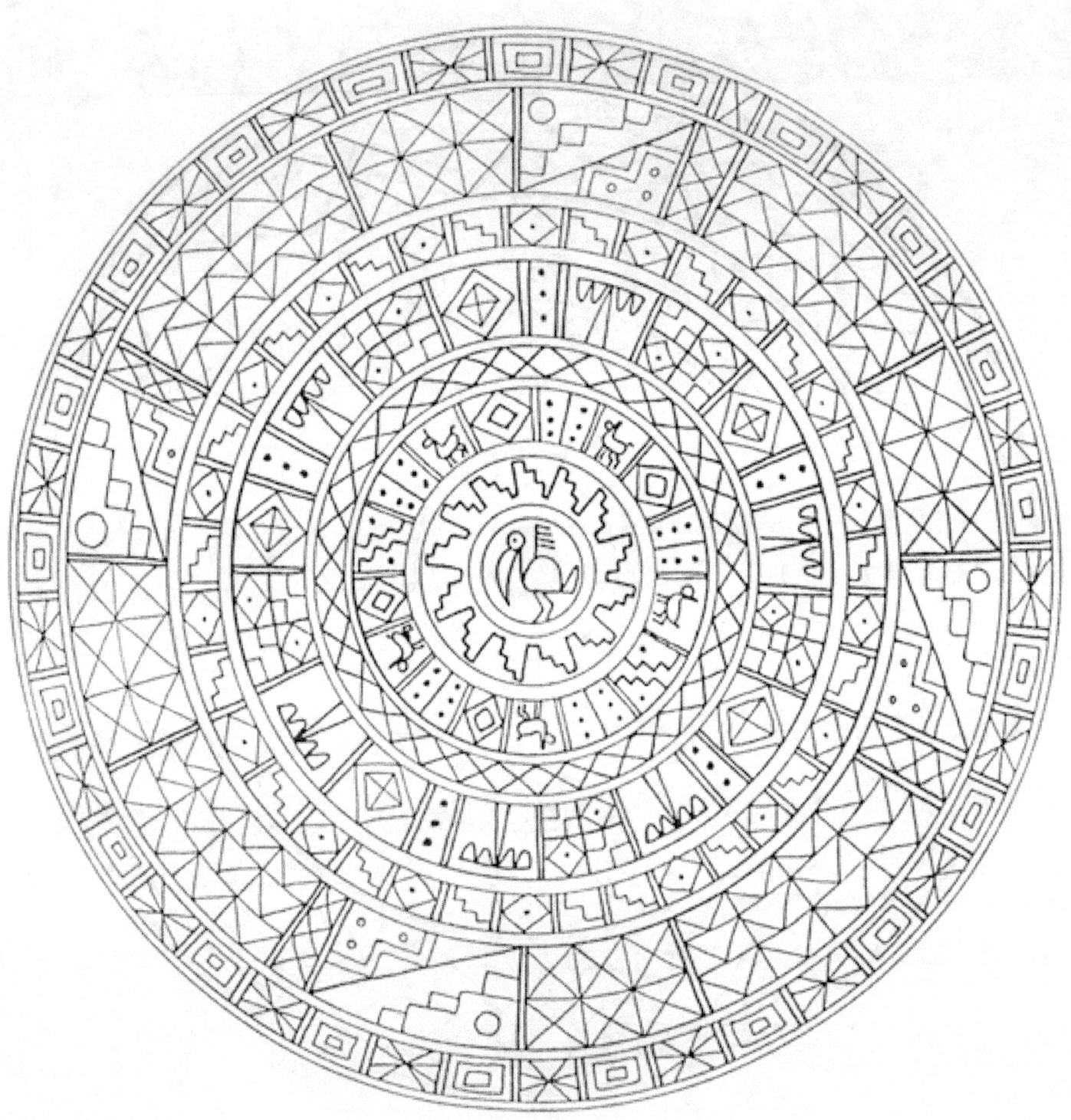

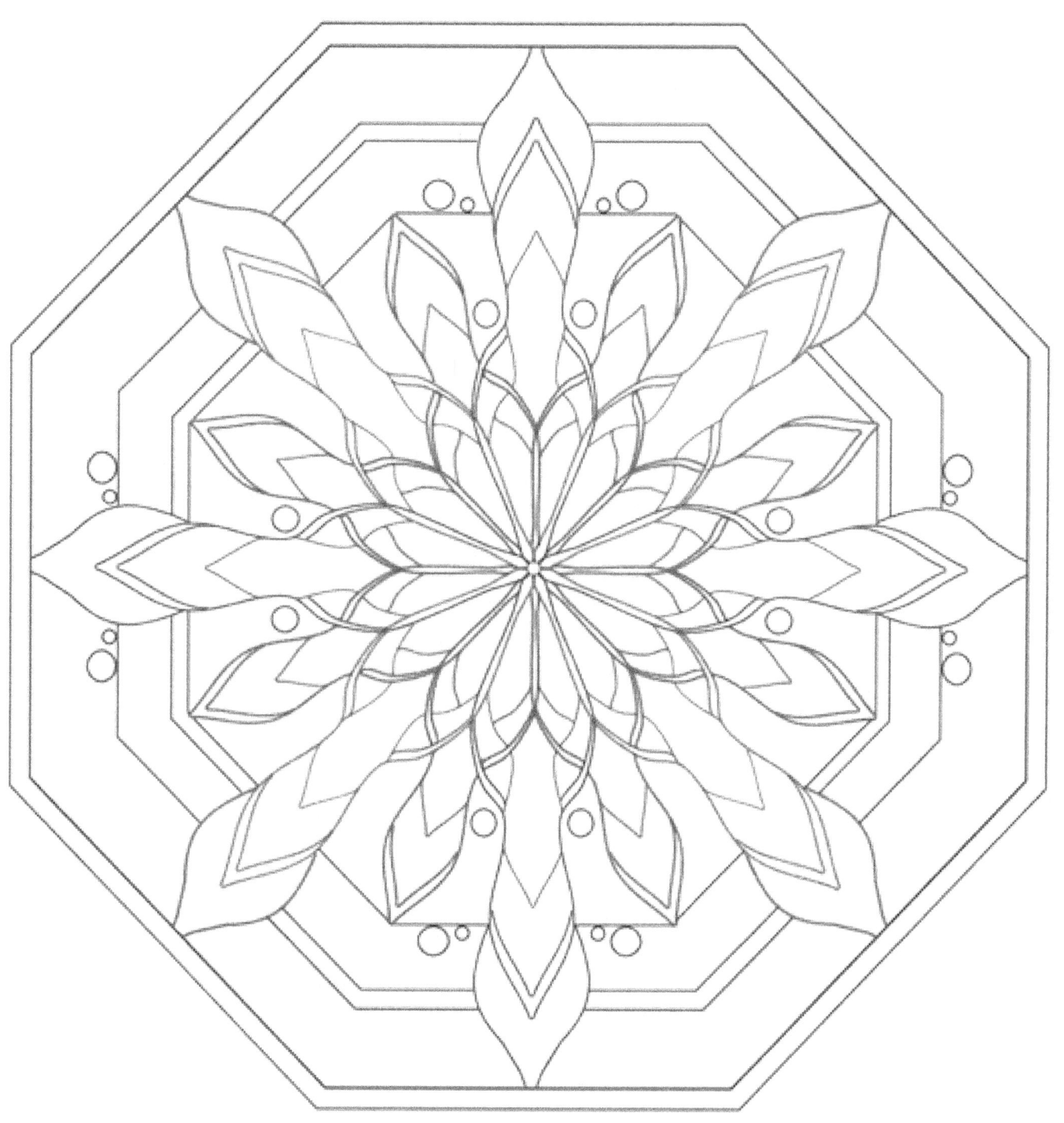

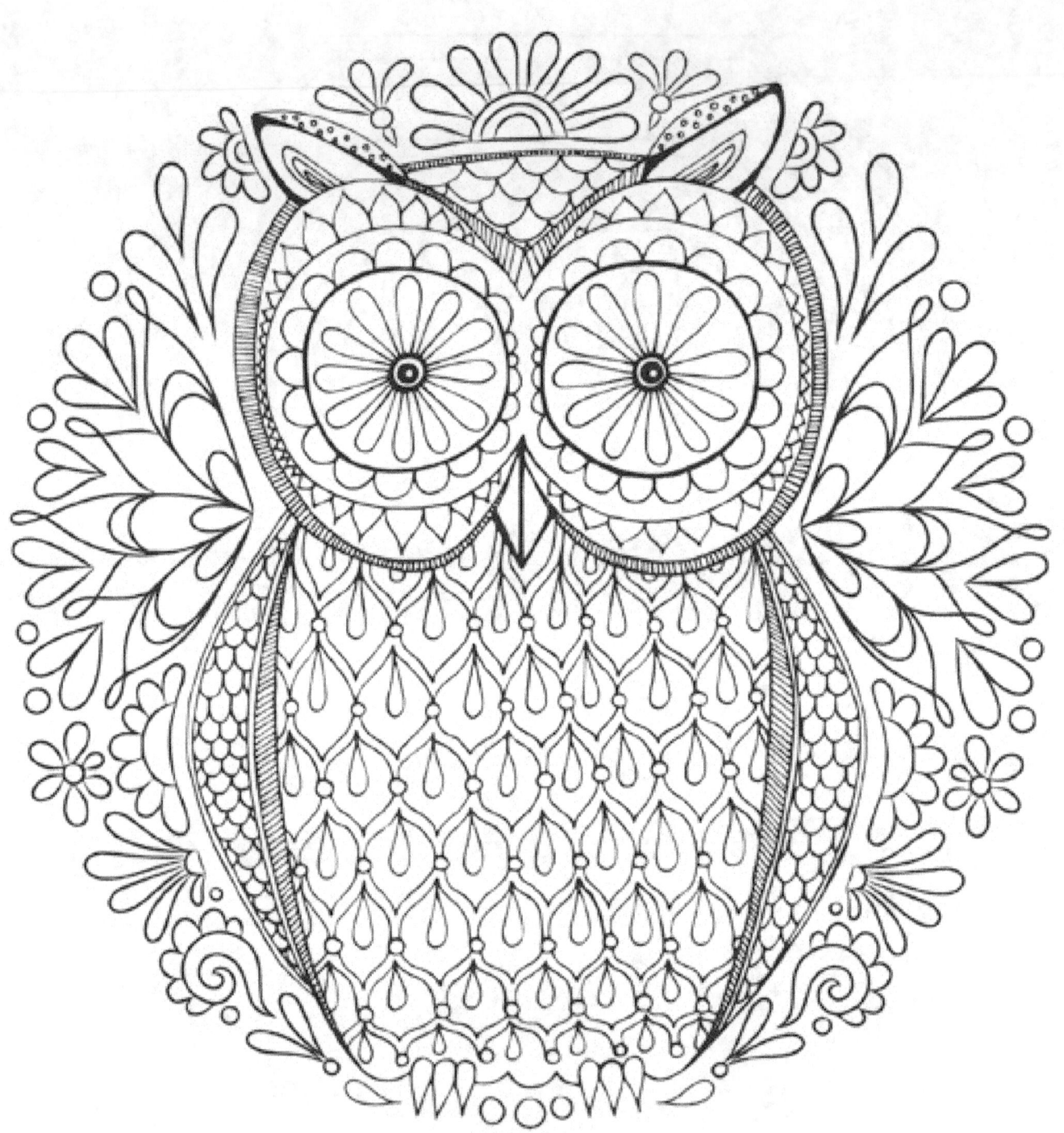

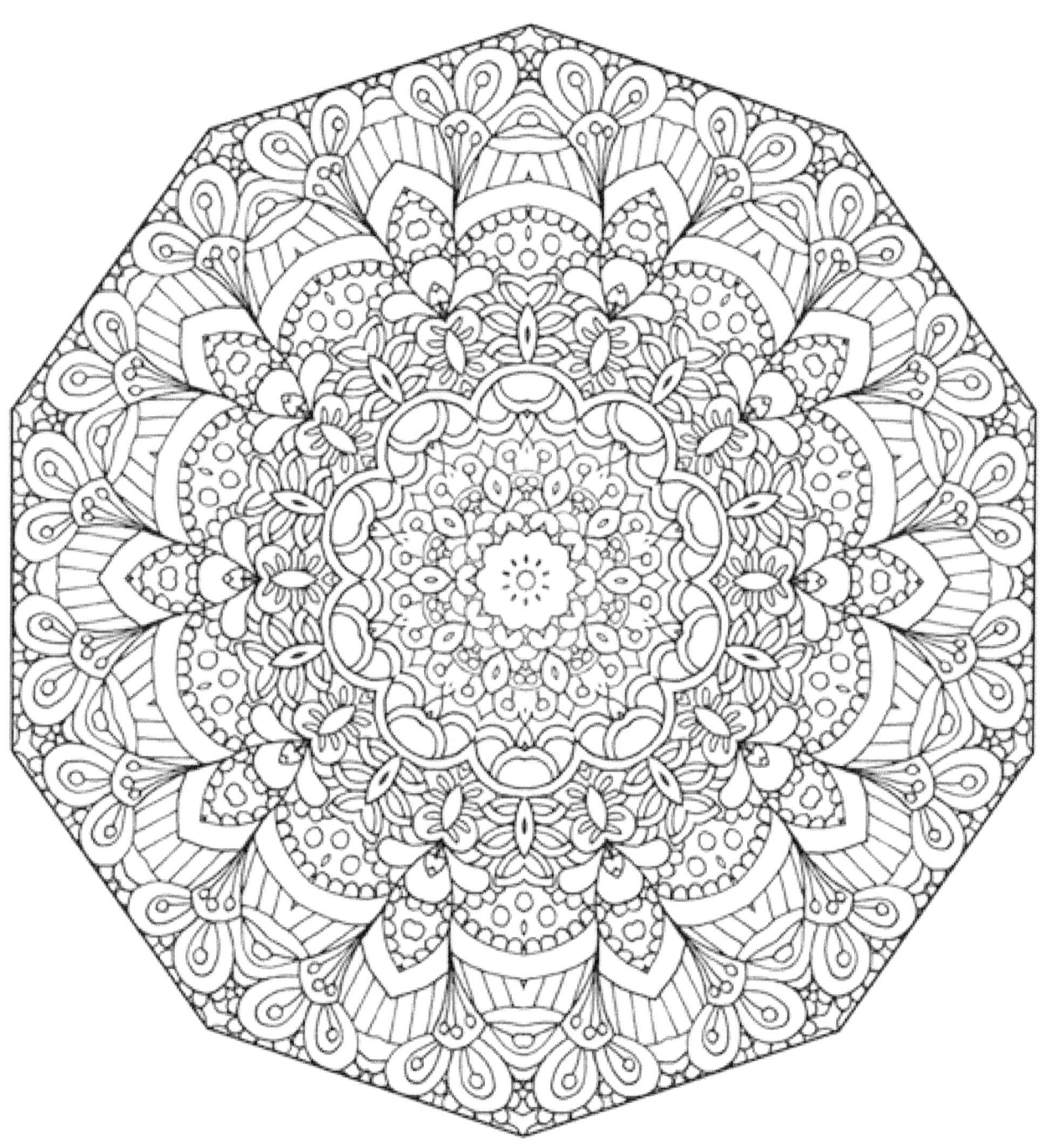

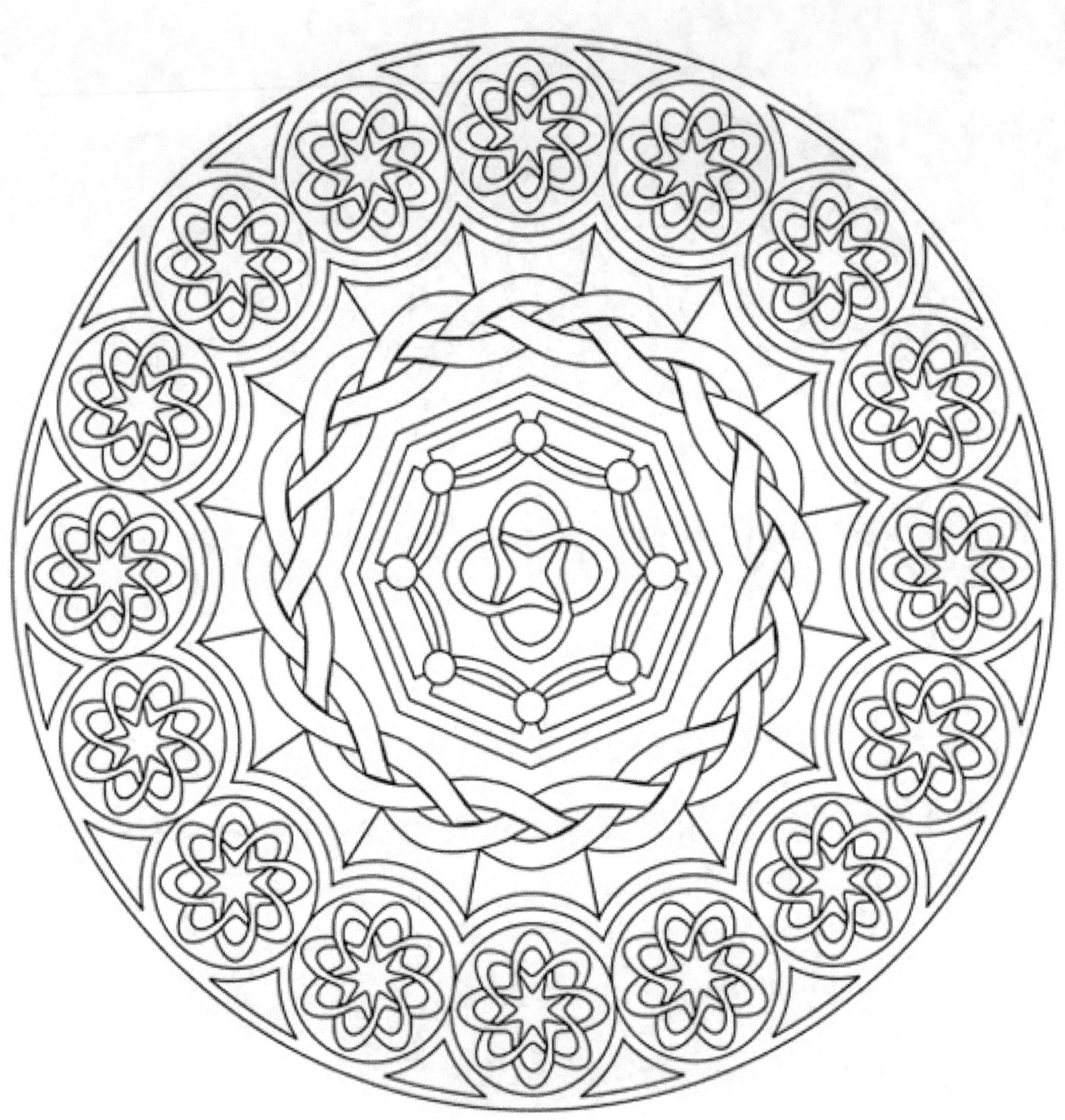